FOR GRADES 7-8

HOW TO GET BETTER TEST SCORES

on Elementary School Standardized Tests

GRADES 7-8

Editor: Jeri Hayes

Design and Production: Lynda Banks Design

Copyright © 1991 by Planned Productions Incorporated

ISBN: 0-679-82110-4

Manufactured in the United States of America

10 9 8 7 6 5 4 3 2 1

Random House New York

Table of Contents

LANGUAGE ARTS
Keeping Track

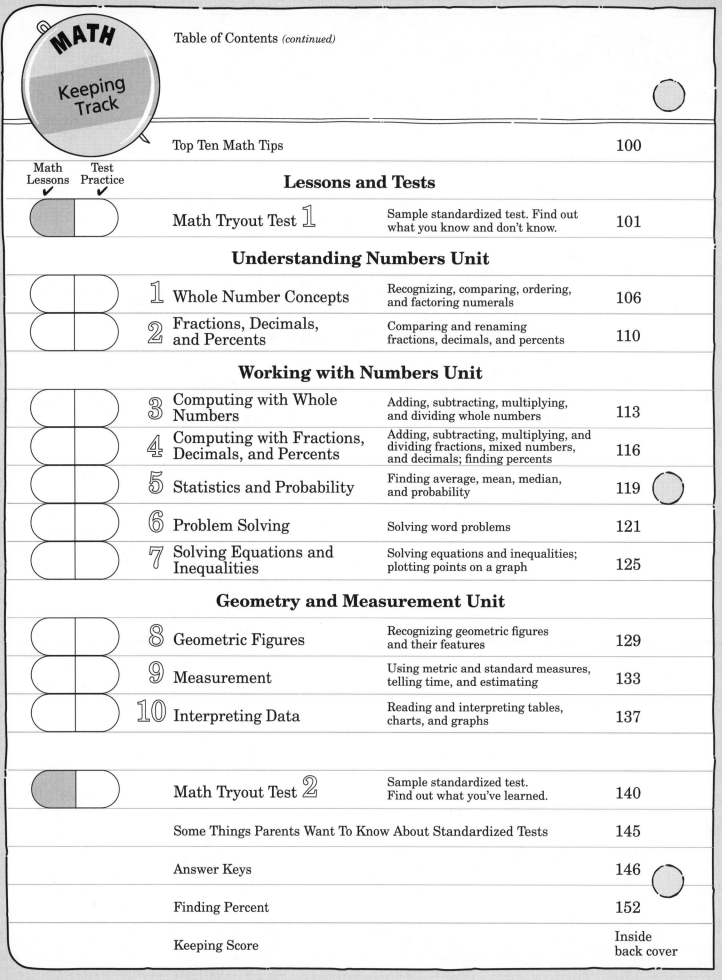

MATH

Keeping Track

Table of Contents *(continued)*

Questions and Answers About Using This Book

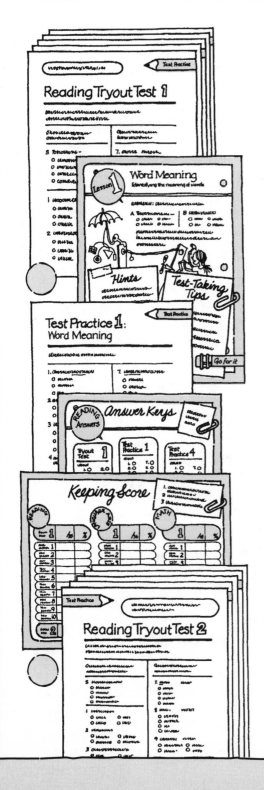

Why is this book so BIG?

Because it's three books in one! Each part gives you practice in a different subject: Reading, Language Arts, and Math.

Do I have to begin with Reading?

No. You can begin with any one of the three parts.

When I have picked a part to start on, how do I start?

Start with Tryout Test 1 for that part. The time needed for the Tryout Test is shown at the top of the first test page.

How do I check my answers?

Find the Answer Keys in the back of the book. When you have totaled the number of questions you got correct, record your score on the test page and on the Keeping Score chart in the back of the book. The page numbers are in the Table of Contents.

Must I do all the lessons in one part of the book before going on to another part?

No. Just be sure to take Tryout Test 1 in each part before you do the lessons in that part. Keep track of what you've done by checking the boxes on the Keeping Track chart found in the Table of Contents.

What do I do when I finish a lesson?

Take the test that goes with that lesson. You don't have to take the test right after you finish the lesson. But if you can, it is a good idea to do one lesson and one test each time you work in your book. To do that, you'll need to plan on one hour of study time. Sometimes, you will finish a lesson and a test in 30 minutes. Other times, you will need the entire hour.

What should I do when I finish a test?

Check your answers and record your score just like you did for the Tryout Test.

What do I do when I finish all the lessons and tests in one part of the book?

Take Tryout Test 2 for that part of the book. Once again, check your answers in the Answer Key and record the number of questions you got correct on the test page and on the Keeping Score chart. Finally, compare your Tryout Test 1 and Tryout Test 2 scores. Then: CELEBRATE!! You are on your way to better test scores and better grades.

Top Ten Test-Taking Tips

Each lesson in this book offers two or more tips that will help you answer the kinds of test questions taught in that lesson. On this page, you will find ten tips that will help you become test-wise, no matter what kind of test you're taking.

1 Work in a quiet, comfortable place where you won't be interrupted by TV or radio, telephones, or talking. Be sure to have plenty of scratch paper and sharp, soft-lead (No. 2) pencils with erasers. You'll also need a bell timer or a clock. When you are ready to begin a test, set the timer, or check the clock, to keep track of the number of minutes the test allows.

2 If you feel nervous before a test, try this: close your eyes and take several slow, deep breaths; spend a few minutes relaxing your mind.

3 When you begin a test, quickly scan all of the questions. This will help you see what the test is about and how many questions you will have to answer.

4 It is important to manage your time while taking a test. Begin by checking the number of questions in the test. Also check the amount of time you have to take the test. Try to complete about half the questions by the time you are about halfway through the total test time.

5 Read all DIRECTIONS through twice. Never begin answering questions before you read the directions.

6 Try to answer ALL the test questions. Do the easy ones first. When you come to a hard question, don't spend a lot of time trying to figure it out. Wait until you have finished all the easy questions, then go back and work on the hard ones.

7 All tests have some hard questions. They are meant to stump you! Don't skip the hard questions. It is much better to guess at the answer. First, find any choices you *know* are wrong. Then look at the leftover choices and make your best guess. Often you will guess right.

8 Mark your answers by filling in the circle with a dark pencil mark. If you make a mistake, erase thoroughly. Then fill in the circle next to the *correct* answer.

9 Stop when you come to the STOP sign at the end of the test, or when your time is up. If you still have time, go back and work on any questions you skipped, or go back and recheck your answers.

10 Remember, we all learn from our mistakes! When your test has been scored, look over the questions you *missed*. Go back and study each one until you know why you missed it. If you still don't understand a question, ask for help.

Reading

Top Ten Reading Tips

1 When asked to answer questions about a reading passage, read the *questions* first. That way, you'll know what to look for as you read the passage. When you finish the passage, go on to answer the questions.

2 In reading questions, look for key words, such as *who*, *what*, *when*, *where*, *why*, and *how*, that tell you what to look for when you read the passage.

3 Practice scanning a reading passage to quickly find key words that will help you answer questions about details.

4 When answering questions about a reading passage, look back at the passage to locate the answer. Don't just rely on your memory.

5 In a reading passage, when you come to a word you don't know, look for context clues: other words in the sentence or paragraph that help to define or explain the unknown word.

6 For fill-in sentences, always read the *entire* sentence before you choose an answer. Use context clues to help you find the answer.

7 When asked to choose a word to complete a sentence, try out all the answer choices in the sentence. Don't rush to fill in the blank; you might get tricked by words that are similar but have different meanings.

8 When looking for word meanings, read all the answer choices carefully. Don't be fooled by words that only *look* or *sound* like the correct answer.

9 When asked to identify order of events, look for key words that signal time sequence, for example: *first, next, then, after, finally,* and *at last*.

10 Watch out for negative words in directions, such as NOT or OPPOSITE. These words tell you exactly what answer to look for. Such words often appear in **bold** or *italic* type, or in ALL CAPITAL LETTERS.

This test will tell you how well you might score on a standardized reading test **before** using this book.

Test Practice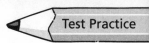

Reading Tryout Test 1

Time: **30** minutes

Directions: Follow the directions for each part of the test. Read each question carefully and fill in the circle beside the answer you choose. The answer to the sample question (**S**) has been filled in for you.

Questions 1–3. Choose the meaning of the underlined word.

S <u>grubby</u> jeans
- Ⓐ old
- Ⓒ cheap
- Ⓑ comfortable
- ● dirty

1. accept the <u>donation</u>
   - Ⓐ scolding
   - Ⓒ letter
   - Ⓑ gift
   - Ⓓ apology

2. <u>divert</u> the river
   - Ⓐ block
   - Ⓒ turn aside
   - Ⓑ make dirty
   - Ⓓ observe

3. the king's <u>sorcerer</u>
   - Ⓐ wizard
   - Ⓒ servant
   - Ⓑ court
   - Ⓓ goblin

Questions 4–5. Fill in the circle next to the definition of the underlined word.

4. <u>computation</u>
   - Ⓐ one who computes
   - Ⓑ not compute
   - Ⓒ compute wrongly
   - Ⓓ the act of computing

5. <u>imperfect</u>
   - Ⓐ the condition of being perfect
   - Ⓑ almost perfect
   - Ⓒ not perfect
   - Ⓓ to make perfect

Questions 6–8. Choose the best answer to each question.

6. Which word most likely comes from the Old French word *jaole*, meaning "cage"?
   - Ⓐ jail
   - Ⓒ jiggle
   - Ⓑ jangle
   - Ⓓ jolt

7. Which word most likely comes from the Arab word *suffa*, meaning "a covered platform"?
   - Ⓐ soft
   - Ⓒ sofa
   - Ⓑ suffrage
   - Ⓓ suffer

8. Which word most likely comes from the Middle English word *masel*, meaning "spot"?
   - Ⓐ maze
   - Ⓒ master
   - Ⓑ measles
   - Ⓓ muscle

Questions 9–11. Choose the word that means the OPPOSITE of the key word.

9. trivial
   - Ⓐ minor
   - Ⓒ difficult
   - Ⓑ important
   - Ⓓ intelligent

10. abundance
    - Ⓐ shortage
    - Ⓒ amount
    - Ⓑ breadth
    - Ⓓ plenty

11. treachery
    - Ⓐ wickedness
    - Ⓒ politeness
    - Ⓑ enemy
    - Ⓓ loyalty

GO ON

Reading Tryout Test 1 (continued)

Questions 12–15. Choose the word that best fits the blank in the sentence.

12. The ship was _____ under a hundred feet of water.
    - Ⓐ submerged
    - Ⓒ sailing
    - Ⓑ floating
    - Ⓓ constructed

13. Nothing stirred on the _____ surface of the lake.
    - Ⓐ liquid
    - Ⓒ violent
    - Ⓑ tranquil
    - Ⓓ dull

14. The ladies' club held a _____ sale to raise money for charity.
    - Ⓐ bankrupt
    - Ⓒ rummage
    - Ⓑ discount
    - Ⓓ percent

15. It took the skiers three days to _____ the glacier.
    - Ⓐ transfer
    - Ⓒ melt
    - Ⓑ domesticate
    - Ⓓ traverse

Questions 16–19. Choose the meaning of the underlined word in each sentence.

16. The apiarist put on protective clothing before going out to work with the hives.
    - Ⓐ insect
    - Ⓑ surgeon
    - Ⓒ beekeeper
    - Ⓓ diver

17. The restaurant manager asked the rambunctious children to calm down.
    - Ⓐ hungry
    - Ⓑ timid
    - Ⓒ lazy
    - Ⓓ wild

18. The mouse was not aware that it was in jeopardy until the cat pounced.
    - Ⓐ hiding
    - Ⓑ danger
    - Ⓒ sickness
    - Ⓓ terror

19. The airplane reached such a high velocity that it broke the sound barrier.
    - Ⓐ speed
    - Ⓑ atmosphere
    - Ⓒ orbit
    - Ⓓ transmission

Questions 20–21. Read the sentence in the box. Then choose the sentence below in which the underlined word is used in the same way.

20.
> A deer stopped to drink from the spring.

   - Ⓐ Daffodils bloom in spring.
   - Ⓑ A spring in the clock broke.
   - Ⓒ She watched the dancer spring high into the air.
   - Ⓓ All of our water comes from a natural spring.

21.
> The photographer shot some beautiful pictures.

   - Ⓐ A hunter heard the shot.
   - Ⓑ Lava shot up from the top of the mountain.
   - Ⓒ Sometimes you have to take a shot and do your best.
   - Ⓓ I shot two rolls of film before the wedding started.

GO ON ➡

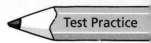
Questions 22–35. Read each passage. Choose the best answer to each question. Fill in the circle beside your answer.

In 1845, farmers in Ireland discovered a white mold on their potato plants. By the following summer, Ireland's main crop was rotting in the fields, and the peasants were beginning to starve. Beginning in 1846 and continuing into the next decade, over a million Irish people were forced to leave their homeland. They traveled to America, but their voyage was a grim one. For the most part, they traveled in cargo ships rather than passenger ships. They passed the voyage in dark, airless spaces far below the deck. These spaces were known as "steerage" because they were located under the back part of the ship, beneath the steering mechanism.

Most of these vessels were sailing ships (rather than the newly invented steamships), so the voyage took six or more weeks. Because diet and hygiene were poor, the emigrants often became ill. Crowded conditions caused diseases to spread quickly and many lives were lost during the voyage, leading the Irish to refer to the vessels as "coffin ships."

Even if passengers were lucky enough to escape serious illness, the voyage was difficult. On most ships, passengers slept in bunkbeds crowded closely together. There was little privacy. Toilet and bathing facilities were inadequate. The ship usually provided meals of bread, potatoes, cereal, and salted fish, but passengers had to bring their own towels, sheets, and blankets. It must have been a huge relief when the passengers spotted land!

22. Which is the best title for this passage?

   Ⓐ "The Great Potato Famine"

   Ⓑ "Arrival in America"

   Ⓒ "The Irish Voyage to America"

   Ⓓ "Sailing Ships of the 1800s"

23. Based on the information in the passage, you can conclude that —

   Ⓐ the potato famine also struck in America

   Ⓑ the Irish immigrants were wealthy

   Ⓒ there had been many potato famines in Ireland

   Ⓓ the Irish saw America as a land of opportunity

24. Which statement from the passage is an opinion?

   Ⓐ In 1845, farmers in Ireland discovered a white mold on their potato plants.

   Ⓑ Their voyage was a grim one.

   Ⓒ The voyage took six or more weeks.

   Ⓓ The ship usually provided meals of bread, potatoes, cereal, and salted fish.

25. In this passage, the author's purpose is to —

   Ⓐ give information about the Irish immigrants

   Ⓑ persuade people to support the Irish immigrants

   Ⓒ entertain with a story about Irish immigrants

   Ⓓ compare the Irish immigrants with the first settlers in America

 GO ON

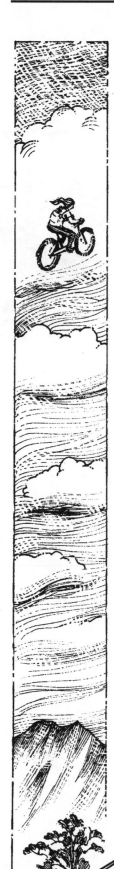

As Mickey bicycled home from the mall, she saw a huge yellow truck at the foot of Orchard Street. Road crews were resurfacing all the streets in her neighborhood. A woman carrying an orange flag motioned Mickey to stop. Gravel gushed out of the truck, and two men with rakes began to spread the stones over the road. Dust filled the air. The flagwoman beckoned to Mickey around the gravel truck. Ahead, a green truck with a large tank was covering the road with asphalt. Mickey peddled quickly to get past the asphalt truck and back into the proper lane. The truck rumbled. The asphalt oozed. Behind her, gravel hissed and clattered. The air was full of fumes and vibrations. With a burst of energy, Mickey nosed past the asphalt truck.

But where was Orchard Street? Instead of finding herself on the dry gray surface of the old road, Mickey discovered that she was — nowhere. It was as if the asphalt truck were an artist drawing a road on a blank piece of paper, and Mickey had suddenly moved ahead of the artist's hand. Mickey shrugged. She thought to herself, "If there's no road, then maybe I can go anywhere." She pulled upwards on the handlebars and the bicycle rose lightly into the air. She laughed and aimed even higher. Within seconds she was hundreds of feet up, looking down on her town.

She could see her father's service station on Main Street, her school on Oak, and the Maple Street Mall where she had just bought some athletic socks. All of these streets were freshly covered with asphalt and gravel. But when she looked up Orchard Street to her family's house, there was no road at all—the trucks hadn't arrived yet. She wiped sweat off her forehead. What she wouldn't give for a glass of lemonade right now! She rode through the air until she was hovering above her home. When she tried to point the bike downwards, nothing happened. A man appeared in the sky in front of her, waving an orange flag around and looking irritated.

"I can't understand you," grumbled Mickey. "Why don't you just tell me what you mean?"

"No bicycles where there are no streets," said the man. "That's the rule."

"But that's my house!" exploded Mickey. " And I'm thirsty! Besides, there was a road here an hour ago."

"You couldn't ride in the air an hour ago, either," replied the man. "Things have changed."

Mickey decided to try some magic. "Alackazam! … Bippedy Boppedy Boo … Open Sesame?" Nothing worked.

Just then the smell of asphalt rose into the air. The green truck was rumbling by, leaving a black shiny path behind it. Then came the gravel truck and the men with the rakes. Mickey's bicycle began slowly sinking and landed gently in front of her driveway.

At the corner of Orchard and Blake, both trucks stopped and the workers took out their lunchboxes. "Just in time!" shouted the flagman in the sky as he disappeared.

GO ON

26. What kind of story is this?

    Ⓐ fantasy

    Ⓑ historical story

    Ⓒ mystery

    Ⓓ animal story

27. How does Mickey feel when her bicycle goes up into the air?

    Ⓐ frightened

    Ⓑ excited

    Ⓒ irritated

    Ⓓ sick

28. What will Mickey most likely do next?

    Ⓐ try to get her bicycle to rise back into the air

    Ⓑ go into the house for a glass of lemonade

    Ⓒ criticize the workers for stopping for lunch

    Ⓓ return to the mall

29. Mickey's main problem in this story is how to —

    Ⓐ get back to the mall

    Ⓑ fly through the air

    Ⓒ ride past the truck

    Ⓓ get to her house

30. What is meant by "It was as if the asphalt truck were an artist drawing a road on a blank piece of paper"?

    Ⓐ The old road was as white as a piece of paper.

    Ⓑ The driver of the asphalt truck worked as carefully as a fine artist.

    Ⓒ No road existed ahead of the asphalt truck.

    Ⓓ The driver of the truck was following instructions on a piece of paper.

31. Which word best describes Mickey?

    Ⓐ artistic

    Ⓑ timid

    Ⓒ lazy

    Ⓓ spunky

32. Which of these events happened first?

    Ⓐ Mickey passed the asphalt truck.

    Ⓑ Mickey reached the foot of Orchard Street.

    Ⓒ Mickey saw her father's service station.

    Ⓓ Mickey bought some athletic socks at the mall.

33. What would have happened if the workers had stopped for lunch before they resurfaced the street in front of Mickey's house?

    Ⓐ Mickey would have eaten lunch with the workers.

    Ⓑ Mickey would have fallen to the ground.

    Ⓒ Mickey would have had to wait to get home.

    Ⓓ Mickey would have found the correct magic word.

34. This story is told by —

    Ⓐ an outside observer

    Ⓑ a girl named Mickey

    Ⓒ a flagman

    Ⓓ Mickey's father

35. In this story, the author's purpose is to —

    Ⓐ teach a lesson

    Ⓑ entertain

    Ⓒ provide information

    Ⓓ persuade

 STOP

Number Correct/Total = _____ /35

13

Word Meaning

Identifying the meaning of words

Directions: Read the phrase. Then choose the word that means the same as the underlined word.

A mimic the actor

- Ⓐ bother
- Ⓑ imitate
- Ⓒ enjoy
- Ⓓ watch

B a strenuous game

- Ⓐ difficult
- Ⓑ exciting
- Ⓒ fair
- Ⓓ popular

In Example A, the underlined word is *mimic*, which means *imitate*. The correct answer is Ⓑ. In Example B, the answer is Ⓐ because *strenuous* means *difficult*.

Improving your vocabulary will help you score better on the Word Meaning part of a test. The best way to learn the meaning of words is to read — stories, magazines, newspapers, letters — even food labels! When you come across words you don't know, look them up in a dictionary.

Another way you can practice learning word meanings is to "mimic" someone who writes dictionaries. Write a definition for a word you know. Then check your definition against the one given in the dictionary.

Test-Taking Tips

1 Try to figure out the meaning of the underlined word before you look at the answer choices.

2 Watch out for words that are closely related but don't have the same meaning. In Example B, *fair* and *popular* are both related to *game*, but neither means the same as *strenuous*.

Go for it

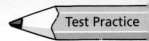

Test Practice 1: Word Meaning

Time: **8** minutes

Directions: Read each phrase. Choose the meaning of the underlined word.

1. a <u>tedious</u> job
   - Ⓐ long
   - Ⓑ important
   - Ⓒ difficult
   - Ⓓ boring

2. <u>confine</u> the dog
   - Ⓐ shut in
   - Ⓑ train
   - Ⓒ treat carefully
   - Ⓓ praise

3. fix the <u>fracture</u>
   - Ⓐ dam
   - Ⓑ furniture
   - Ⓒ mistake
   - Ⓓ break

4. <u>delude</u> the voters
   - Ⓐ appeal to
   - Ⓑ mislead
   - Ⓒ disappoint
   - Ⓓ count

5. <u>activate</u> the alarm
   - Ⓐ put in
   - Ⓑ ignore
   - Ⓒ turn on
   - Ⓓ notice

6. <u>scrumptious</u> berries
   - Ⓐ delicious
   - Ⓑ rotten
   - Ⓒ scarlet
   - Ⓓ poisonous

7. made of <u>wicker</u>
   - Ⓐ iron
   - Ⓑ boards
   - Ⓒ plastic
   - Ⓓ twigs

8. widely <u>prohibited</u>
   - Ⓐ permissible
   - Ⓑ attended
   - Ⓒ forbidden
   - Ⓓ criticized

9. an <u>inquisitive</u> child
   - Ⓐ naughty
   - Ⓑ curious
   - Ⓒ helpful
   - Ⓓ loyal

10. discover the <u>hoax</u>
    - Ⓐ trick
    - Ⓑ criminal
    - Ⓒ present
    - Ⓓ secret

11. a <u>dank</u> room
    - Ⓐ large and attractive
    - Ⓑ comfortable
    - Ⓒ damp and cold
    - Ⓓ airless

12. <u>wheedle</u> her
    - Ⓐ coax
    - Ⓑ help
    - Ⓒ disobey
    - Ⓓ remember

Number Correct/Total = _____ /12

15

Word Analysis

Recognizing prefixes, suffixes, and root words

Directions: Choose the meaning of the key word.

A nameless

   Ⓐ like a name

   Ⓑ without a name

   Ⓒ before a name

   Ⓓ name wrongly

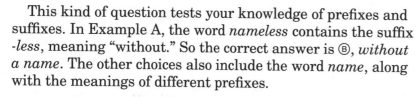

This kind of question tests your knowledge of prefixes and suffixes. In Example A, the word *nameless* contains the suffix *-less*, meaning "without." So the correct answer is Ⓑ, *without a name*. The other choices also include the word *name*, along with the meanings of different prefixes.

Here are some of the common prefixes and suffixes.

Prefixes: re-, pre-, dis-, anti-, trans-, im-, in-, de-, ex-, inter-
Suffixes: -less, -ful, -ment, -ation, -able, -ness, -er, -al, -ical

Now look at this example.

B Directions: Which word most likely comes from the Latin word *carta*, meaning "paper"?

   Ⓐ cart   Ⓒ career

   Ⓑ cardinal Ⓓ cartoon

This kind of question tests your knowledge of root words. The Latin word *carta* means "paper." The modern English word *cartoon* comes from the Latin root, *carta*. Choice Ⓓ is the only one that is related to "paper," and the spelling is similar to *carta*.

Test-Taking Tips

1 To find the meaning of the key word, first separate the root word from the prefix or suffix. (Nameless = *name* + *less*). Then look for the meaning of the prefix or suffix in the answer choices.

2 To find the modern word that comes from the root, look for the word that is closest in meaning and in spelling (as in *cartoon*, which is drawn on *paper*).

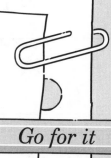

Go for it

Test Practice 2: Word Analysis

Time: **8** minutes

Questions 1–8. Read the key word. Choose the meaning.

1. resignation

   Ⓐ not resign

   Ⓑ resign again

   Ⓒ able to resign

   Ⓓ the act of resigning

2. employer

   Ⓐ the state of being employed

   Ⓑ one who employs

   Ⓒ like employing

   Ⓓ employ wrongly

3. impractical

   Ⓐ the condition of being practical

   Ⓑ in a practical manner

   Ⓒ not practical

   Ⓓ to make practical

4. finality

   Ⓐ to make final

   Ⓑ not final

   Ⓒ the state of being final

   Ⓓ final again

5. predesign

   Ⓐ design again

   Ⓑ design through

   Ⓒ something that designs

   Ⓓ design in advance

6. transcontinental

   Ⓐ across the continent

   Ⓑ under the continent

   Ⓒ over the continent

   Ⓓ half a continent

7. believable

   Ⓐ not believe

   Ⓑ able to be believed

   Ⓒ the state of believing

   Ⓓ without belief

8. interoffice

   Ⓐ within the office

   Ⓑ across the office

   Ⓒ between offices

   Ⓓ before the office

Questions 9–12. Choose the word that best answers each question.

9. Which word most likely comes from the Old English word *mor*, meaning "wasteland"?

   Ⓐ month   Ⓒ morning

   Ⓑ moor   Ⓓ morsel

10. Which word most likely comes from the Greek word *kaminos*, meaning "oven"?

    Ⓐ chimney   Ⓒ camel

    Ⓑ caramel   Ⓓ chime

11. Which word most likely comes from the Spanish word *barbacoa*, meaning "pile of sticks"?

    Ⓐ barber   Ⓒ bargain

    Ⓑ bareback   Ⓓ barbeque

12. Which word most likely comes from the Latin word *terra*, meaning "land"?

    Ⓐ terrify   Ⓒ terrible

    Ⓑ territory   Ⓓ terry cloth

STOP

Number Correct/Total = _____ /12

17

Synonyms and Antonyms

Recognizing synonyms and antonyms

happy
joyful
elated

unhappy
sorrowful
depressed

Directions: Choose the word that means the same, or nearly the same, as the key word.

A accumulate

- Ⓐ gather
- Ⓑ stack
- Ⓒ provide
- Ⓓ count

Directions: Choose the word that means the OPPOSITE of the key word.

B tumult

- Ⓐ excitement
- Ⓑ battle
- Ⓒ calm
- Ⓓ terror

Example A tests your knowledge of synonyms. **Synonyms** are words that have the same, or nearly the same, meanings. The synonym for *accumulate* is *gather*, answer Ⓐ.

Example B tests your knowledge of **antonyms**, which are words with opposite meanings. The opposite of *tumult* is *calm*, answer Ⓒ.

Hints

You can practice with synonyms and antonyms in your writing. Next time you have a writing assignment, circle all your "dull" words and list several more colorful words that mean the same. Then see if you can list antonyms for each of the synonyms you wrote. For example, a dull word might be *sad*. Here are some colorful synonyms for *sad*: forlorn, sorrowful, gloomy, downhearted, crestfallen, despondent, morose, desolate, melancholy. Now can you give an antonym for each of those synonyms? Try it.

Get to know your thesaurus! This helpful reference book lists hundreds of synonyms and antonyms. Need a colorful synonym for any word? Check your thesaurus!

Test-Taking Tips

1 Watch out for words that are related to the key word but are not true synonyms or antonyms. In Example A, both *stack* and *count* could be related to *accumulate*, but neither is a synonym.

2 When you are looking for a synonym, watch out for opposites. When you are looking for an antonym, watch out for words that mean the same. In Example B, *excitement* is a synonym for *tumult*.

Go for it

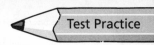

Test Practice 3: Synonyms and Antonyms

Time: 8 minutes

Questions 1–6. Choose the word that means the same, or nearly the same, as the key word.

1. tussle
   - Ⓐ bother
   - Ⓑ fight
   - Ⓒ hill
   - Ⓓ hug

2. aloof
   - Ⓐ awkward
   - Ⓑ polite
   - Ⓒ dry
   - Ⓓ unfriendly

3. pavilion
   - Ⓐ tent
   - Ⓑ sidewalk
   - Ⓒ village
   - Ⓓ bell

4. apparition
   - Ⓐ wall
   - Ⓑ ghost
   - Ⓒ idea
   - Ⓓ rule

5. ingenious
   - Ⓐ dull
   - Ⓑ inexperienced
   - Ⓒ stupid
   - Ⓓ clever

6. maul
   - Ⓐ shop
   - Ⓑ help
   - Ⓒ injure
   - Ⓓ feed

Questions 7–12. Choose the word that means the OPPOSITE of the key word.

7. synthetic
   - Ⓐ fake
   - Ⓑ expensive
   - Ⓒ natural
   - Ⓓ chemical

8. plummet
   - Ⓐ skip
   - Ⓑ rise
   - Ⓒ devour
   - Ⓓ fall

9. futile
   - Ⓐ successful
   - Ⓑ weak
   - Ⓒ wealthy
   - Ⓓ sturdy

10. aggressive
    - Ⓐ selfish
    - Ⓑ gentle
    - Ⓒ proud
    - Ⓓ generous

11. virtue
    - Ⓐ saint
    - Ⓑ gift
    - Ⓒ cowardice
    - Ⓓ evil

12. deplore
    - Ⓐ approve
    - Ⓑ dissolve
    - Ⓒ pity
    - Ⓓ increase

Number Correct/Total = _____ /12

19

Context Clues

Using context clues to find word meanings
and to define multiple-meaning words

Directions: Choose the word that best fits the blank.

A Devon's stomach knotted as the nurse gave him a shot. The sight of a needle made him _____.

   Ⓐ angry   Ⓒ wounded

   Ⓑ courageous   Ⓓ squeamish

This kind of question tests your ability to use context clues to find a missing word. **Context clues** are other words in the sentence or sentences that can help you understand word meaning. In Example A, the most important clue is that Devon "closed his eyes" so he would not see the needle. This clue suggests that needles make Devon feel *squeamish*, choice Ⓓ. He certainly did not feel *angry* or *courageous*, and the sight of a needle would not make him *wounded*.

Now look at this example.

Directions: Choose the meaning of the underlined word in the sentence.

B The rest of the guests stared at the woman who <u>guzzled</u> her water noisily and then slammed her empty glass on the table.

   Ⓐ noticed   Ⓒ gulped

   Ⓑ refused   Ⓓ sipped

To answer this kind of question, you have to use context clues to figure out the meaning of an unfamiliar word. In Example B, there are several clues to the meaning of *guzzled*. It involves water, and it is noisy. After the woman guzzles her water, her glass is empty. If you put all these clues together, you can figure out that *guzzled* means *gulped*, choice Ⓒ. The other choices do not fit the context of the sentence.

Now look at this example.

Directions: Read the sentence in the box. Then choose the sentence below in which the underlined word is used in the same way.

C | The water skier leaped across the boat's <u>wake</u>.

SPEED DEMON

   Ⓐ Please don't <u>wake</u> up your father.

   Ⓑ The mayor will attend the <u>wake</u> for the police chief.

   Ⓒ <u>Wake</u> up before you run the car off the road!

   Ⓓ Our little rowboat bobbed in the <u>wake</u> of the ferry.

This kind of question uses **multiple-meaning words**, or words with several different meanings. Some of the meanings are also different parts of speech. In the sentence in the box, *wake* refers to the "trail left by a boat." The sentence in choice Ⓓ uses *wake* in the same way. The other choices are incorrect because they use different meanings of *wake*. In choices Ⓐ and Ⓒ, *wake* is also used as a different part of speech.

Hints

Here are some examples of different kinds of context clues which can help you find the meaning of a word.

Clues	Examples
▶ **Definition**	We drove by a <u>hogan</u>, a Navajo dwelling made of earth and wooden timbers.
▶ **Description**	Mr. Slattery is a terrible <u>misanthrope</u>; he dislikes his co-workers, his neighbors, and even his own family.
▶ **Examples**	At the party there were dozens of <u>hors d'oeuvres</u>, including cheese and crackers, olives, stuffed mushrooms, and vegetables with dip.
▶ **Synonyms**	The scientist studied the <u>carapace</u>, or shell, of the turtle.
▶ **Antonyms**	Bill looked <u>rapturous</u> when he received a new skateboard; his mother, on the other hand, looked displeased.
▶ **Comparison** *or* **Contrast**	Lee was very <u>gregarious</u>; this was not surprising, since everyone in his family enjoyed meeting and talking with new people.
	The library was <u>tenebrous</u> until somebody opened the curtains and let the sunshine in.

Test-Taking Tips

1 Context clues may not be in the same sentence as the underlined word or the blank. Look at the sentences before and after it, too. (In Example A, you need clues from both sentences to determine that *squeamish* is the best choice.)

2 Before you look at the answer choices, try to figure out the meaning of the word that is missing or underlined.

3 For context clues: Try out your answer choice in the sentence to see if it makes sense. Watch out for words that seem to fit the sentence, but do not fit the context clues exactly. (In Example B, the woman might have *sipped* her water noisily, but "sipping" does not fit the context of "the guests stared" and "slammed her empty glass.")

4 For multiple-meaning words: Decide what the underlined word means in the first sentence, then try out the same meaning in the other sentences. Make sure the sentence uses the word as the same part of speech (as in "the wake" as compared to "to wake").

Go for it

21

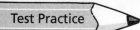

Test Practice 4 : Context Clues

Time: **14** minutes

Questions 1–5. Choose the word that best fits the blank in each sentence.

1. Poncho could see nothing but grass in every direction on the _____ prairie.

   Ⓐ inviting   Ⓒ boundless

   Ⓑ burning   Ⓓ narrow

2. I can't let this feud continue; I've got to _____ him today.

   Ⓐ confront   Ⓒ discuss

   Ⓑ threaten   Ⓓ please

3. Dr. Cohn has never been able to catch the _____ swallowtail butterfly.

   Ⓐ wonderful   Ⓒ determined

   Ⓑ elusive   Ⓓ wandering

4. We waited for the _____ to show us to our table in the café.

   Ⓐ usher   Ⓒ chef

   Ⓑ conductor   Ⓓ hostess

5. The elf king's _____ says that a human will save the kingdom from this evil threat.

   Ⓐ prophecy   Ⓒ ring

   Ⓑ legislation   Ⓓ chant

Questions 6–10. Choose the meaning of the underlined word in each sentence.

6. To escape the sheriff's men, Robin Hood urged his horse down the hill and into the shade of the <u>dingle</u>.

   Ⓐ mountaintop   Ⓒ river's edge

   Ⓑ meadow   Ⓓ wooded valley

7. Sian can't make up her mind about whether or not to go to summer camp; she keeps <u>vacillating</u>.

   Ⓐ packing   Ⓒ explaining

   Ⓑ wavering   Ⓓ pretending

8. This poetry book is a real <u>miscellany</u> of different styles.

   Ⓐ mixture   Ⓒ binding

   Ⓑ verse   Ⓓ preface

9. That dreadful smell came from a <u>putrefied</u> orange that had been under the refrigerator for weeks.

   Ⓐ large   Ⓒ beautiful

   Ⓑ dried   Ⓓ rotten

10. Margo and Skip plan to race their <u>catamaran</u> across the lake this weekend.

   Ⓐ bicycle   Ⓒ swimmer

   Ⓑ boat   Ⓓ small

GO ON

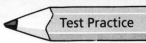

Questions 11–16. Read the sentence in the box. Then choose the sentence below that uses the underlined word in the same way.

11.

> I forgot to bring any money; luckily, the concert was <u>free</u>.

Ⓐ Three days later, the road was finally <u>free</u> of debris.

Ⓑ Alicia is <u>free</u> to use her neighbors' pool anytime.

Ⓒ When Joel finishes his work, the computer will be <u>free</u>.

Ⓓ Entrance to the fair is <u>free</u>, but all the rides are quite expensive.

12.

> The architect drew a dark <u>line</u> across the floor plan.

Ⓐ Every time I call the garage, the <u>line</u> is busy.

Ⓑ Once you cross the <u>line</u> into Canada, you have to obey Canadian law.

Ⓒ Mom scolded him for drawing a <u>line</u> on the wallpaper.

Ⓓ Candy felt a tug on the <u>line</u> and started to reel it in.

13.

> Sales went up when the restaurant <u>cut</u> its prices.

Ⓐ The factory owners <u>cut</u> the workers' salaries.

Ⓑ <u>Cut</u> the cranberry juice with grapefruit juice so it is not so sweet.

Ⓒ Brett <u>cut</u> his foot on a piece of barbed wire.

Ⓓ The coach <u>cut</u> Dwayne from the team.

14.

> Our piano needs to be tuned; several of the notes are <u>flat</u>.

Ⓐ We were late to the party because we got a <u>flat</u> tire.

Ⓑ Somebody left the cap off the bottle; the soda went <u>flat</u>.

Ⓒ The Midwest is really not <u>flat</u>; much of it has rolling hills.

Ⓓ If the tune sounds too <u>flat</u>, try changing the key.

15.

> Do you have the sales <u>figure</u> for last month?

Ⓐ This <u>figure</u> is a lot lower than I expected.

Ⓑ Mom does aerobic exercises to keep her <u>figure</u>.

Ⓒ You can <u>figure</u> out the answer by following the procedure for solving equations.

Ⓓ But that doesn't <u>figure</u>; he said he'd be here early.

16.

> The shopper handed a <u>check</u> to the salesclerk.

Ⓐ The police ran a <u>check</u> on the car's license plate.

Ⓑ The jacket is beige with a dark brown <u>check</u>.

Ⓒ The Ferraros always pay the babysitter with a <u>check</u>.

Ⓓ The teacher put a <u>check</u> next to the name of each student who got on the bus.

Number Correct/Total = _____ /16

Main Idea and Details

Finding the main idea and supporting details in a reading passage

Directions: Read the passage. Choose the best answer to each question.

If you know when and where to look, you can observe badgers in the wild. These creatures like to dig their large underground burrows in fairly dry, sandy soil. They usually pick sites that are covered with some kind of vegetation — anything from trees to low bushes. This cover protects the badgers from being seen easily as they enter or leave their burrows. Burrows are usually located near water and often near wild berries, which badgers love to eat.

Once you have located a burrow, determine which openings are currently in use. (Some burrows have as many as fifty entrances!) Fresh tracks at the mouth of an opening are a good indicator of recent activity.

Badgers are most active at night, so it is best to begin your observation in the early evening. Make sure you arrive at about sunset, before the badgers begin to emerge from their tunnels. Pick a spot about ten feet from a well-used entry, and climb a tree if possible. If you are above the ground, you will be able to see the animals better and they are less likely to notice you. Try to position yourself so that the wind is not coming from behind you; you don't want it to blow your scent toward the badgers and frighten them. Once you have found a good spot, stay as still and quiet as possible. Soon the badgers will wake up and come out to eat.

A Which is the best title for this passage?

Ⓐ "Finding Burrows"

Ⓑ "The Habits of Badgers"

Ⓒ "Animals of the Night"

Ⓓ "Looking for Badgers"

B Where do badgers live?

Ⓐ in underground burrows

Ⓑ under water

Ⓒ in the branches of trees

Ⓓ inside rocky caves

C The best time to observe badgers is at about —

Ⓐ noon

Ⓑ sunset

Ⓒ midnight

Ⓓ dawn

D Which sentence best supports the main idea of this passage?

Ⓐ Some burrows have as many as fifty entrances!

Ⓑ Badgers love to eat berries.

Ⓒ If you are above the ground, you will be able to see the animals better.

Ⓓ This cover protects the badgers from being seen easily.

Questions about the **main idea** may ask you to choose the best title, the main topic, or the main idea statement. They may ask for the main idea of the whole passage or of just one paragraph. To answer these questions, you have to decide what the passage, or a certain paragraph, is mainly about.

The passage you have just read is mainly about where and when to look for badgers. The main idea is stated in the first sentence of the passage: "If you know where and when to look, you can observe badgers in the wild." Example A asks you to choose the best title for the passage, so the answer is Ⓓ, "Looking for Badgers." The other choices are based on details in the passage, but they do not express the main idea.

Other questions ask about **factual details** in the passage. These details give information about the topic and can be verified as facts. In Example B, the answer is Ⓐ, *in underground burrows*. The second sentence states that badgers "like to dig their underground burrows in fairly dry, sandy soil." The rest of the paragraph describes the burrow.

Example C asks about the best time to see a badger. The answer to this question is Ⓑ, *sunset*. It is stated in the first sentence of the last paragraph: "Badgers are most active at night, so it is best to begin your observation in the early evening."

Other questions ask you to find **supporting details**. These are details which support, or illustrate, the main idea of the passage. Example D asks for the detail that best supports the main idea of the passage. All of the choices are details from the passage, but choice Ⓒ best supports the main idea: where and when to look for a badger.

Test-Taking Tips

1 Read the whole passage carefully to decide what the passage is mainly about. Sometimes a passage contains a single sentence that states the main idea. Sometimes the main idea is suggested by two or more sentences.

2 The main idea is most often at the beginning of a passage or paragraph, but it will sometimes appear in the middle or at the end.

3 Don't confuse detail sentences with main ideas. The main idea is usually a general statement; details contain specific facts.

4 Questions about factual details usually ask about the "Four W's": *who, when, what,* and *where*. These are good things to look for as you read.

Go for it

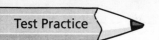

Test Practice 5: Main Idea and Details
Time: **8** minutes

Directions: *Questions 1–8.* Read each passage. Choose the best answer to each question.

Human beings have always suffered from nightmares, but scientists are now beginning to understand a little about how these dreams work. Human sleep can be divided into two stages. Most sleep is known as S-sleep, and during this phase the body gradually relaxes. Then the individual enters what is called D-sleep. During D-sleep, the body is very relaxed, but the brain becomes extremely active. Dreams occur during D-sleep.

Everybody dreams (whether or not they remember doing so), but not everybody has nightmares. Recent studies suggest that about half of the population has nightmares once in a while, while about 5% of adults have nightmares more than once a week.

There are two basic types of nightmares. In the standard nightmare, the dreamer is always frightenened by something, but the threat changes: one night it may be a monster from outer space, the next night a TV villain. Another kind of dream repeats, in unchanging detail, a disturbing real-life experience, such as an automobile accident. The first type of nightmare is difficult to treat, but the second kind can sometimes be eliminated by having the dreamer talk about the experience.

According to the director of a sleep laboratory in Boston, frequent nightmare sufferers are different from other people. They tend to be rebellious and artistic. They have unusually good memories of the past and are very sensitive to the emotions of others. However, in most ways, they are ordinary people. They go to work. They have normal relationships with others. They cannot be easily identified.

1. What is this passage mostly about?

   Ⓐ individuals who suffer from frequent nightmares

   Ⓑ the differences between S-sleep and D-sleep

   Ⓒ scientific discoveries about nightmares

   Ⓓ treatment for people who suffer from nightmares

2. About what percent of adults suffer from nightmares more than once a week?

   Ⓐ 5%   Ⓒ 25%

   Ⓑ 10%   Ⓓ 50%

3. People who dream repeatedly about a real-life experience can often be helped if they —

   Ⓐ take medicine   Ⓒ sleep less

   Ⓑ become artists   Ⓓ talk about it

4. Which detail best supports the main idea of the last paragraph?

   Ⓐ They have unusually good memories of the past.

   Ⓑ They go to work.

   Ⓒ They are ordinary people.

   Ⓓ They have normal relationships.

 GO ON

In 1680, English settlers in Maryland complained they had so little food that they had to resort to eating oysters. Soon they stopped complaining and started to regard oysters as a delicacy. The Chesapeake Bay supported a huge oyster fishery, and nobody saw any reason to limit the number of oysters caught.

The yearly catch was greatest in 1885, but then it began to drop. Today, fishermen who have made a living on oysters mourn that the industry is almost dead. Few oysters are left, and those that remain are sick.

The problem began with overfishing: oysters were caught in such great numbers that the remaining oysters couldn't reproduce fast enough to keep up with the demand. Oysters live in clusters on reefs. When an oyster bed is stripped of all oysters, the other creatures that live on the reef die, too. Then, even if oysters can be raised somewhere else, they can never be returned to that bed. The complex balance among numerous life forms has been destroyed forever.

Another problem is pollution. Scientists have measured 70,000 poisons in the Chesapeake. Some of them kill oysters directly. Others just weaken them.

The weakened survivors are now under attack by a disease known as MSX. Scientists do not know where this disease has come from, but they know that unless they find oysters able to resist it, the Chesapeake will soon be empty of oysters.

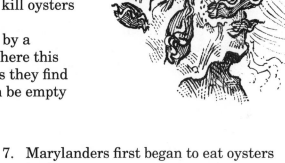

5. What is the main idea of this passage?

   Ⓐ For centuries, oyster fishing has been an important industry in Chesapeake Bay.

   Ⓑ The oysters that live in the Chesapeake today are ill.

   Ⓒ Overfishing, pollution, and disease have combined to endanger the oysters of the Chesapeake.

   Ⓓ When a bed is stripped of its oysters, it is destroyed forever.

6. What is MSX?

   Ⓐ a disease

   Ⓑ a type of pollution

   Ⓒ a type of oyster

   Ⓓ food for oysters

7. Marylanders first began to eat oysters in the —

   Ⓐ 1600s

   Ⓑ 1700s

   Ⓒ 1800s

   Ⓓ 1900s

8. When an oyster bed is stripped of all its oysters, what happens to the other creatures that lived on the oyster bed?

   Ⓐ They move to another reef.

   Ⓑ They multiply rapidly.

   Ⓒ They die.

   Ⓓ They are harvested by fishermen.

Number Correct/Total = _____ /8

27

READING Lesson 6

Constructing Meaning

Relating ideas to interpret the meaning of a reading passage

Directions: Read the passage. Choose the best answer to each question.

Ping! Mara and her friend Sandy ducked. The bus had just left the school and already the kids in the back of the bus had started to throw things. It was always the same group: Lenny J., Priscilla, Anita, and Sam. They tormented everybody on the bus, but somehow the driver never noticed them and nobody was brave enough to report them. The group had made it clear that there were lots of ways to get revenge.

"Hey, Mara," yelled Sam. "Hey, Potato Head. What's with the pajamas?"

Mara blushed. Sam was the worst, because all of his insults were so close to the truth. Mara was sure that her head was unusually long and shaped like one of those Idaho baking potatoes. She blushed again because he had made fun of her new red-and-white striped jumpsuit. She would never wear it again. She ducked her head, hoping Sam would ignore her.

"Yo, Sandy," called Anita. "Where'd you get the worms in your ears?"

Sandy laughed and yelled back, "You should be so lucky as to have earrings this nice. Give up, Anita, you'll never be as nasty as Sam no matter how hard you try."

This time it was Anita's turn to look embarrassed.

A What happened right after the bus left the school?

  Ⓐ Sam teased Mara.

  Ⓑ Anita teased Sandy.

  Ⓒ The bus driver noticed what the group was doing.

  Ⓓ The group began throwing things.

B How are Mara and Sandy different?

  Ⓐ Mara is wilder than Sandy.

  Ⓑ Mara is crueler than Sandy.

  Ⓒ Sandy is bolder than Mara.

  Ⓓ Sandy is less confident than Mara.

C Why don't the other students on the bus report the gang to the bus driver?

  Ⓐ They don't notice the group's behavior.

  Ⓑ They are afraid of the group.

  Ⓒ They are misbehaving, too.

  Ⓓ They think the driver will punish everybody.

D Mara blushed at Sam's comments because she —

  Ⓐ felt self-conscious

  Ⓑ liked Sam a lot

  Ⓒ knew the bus driver had heard them

  Ⓓ was younger than Sam

In every passage, or text, that you read, ideas are related to one another in some way. In some passages, the relationships between ideas are stated clearly. In other passages, the relationships are *implied*, or suggested, and you have to read carefully to figure out what the writer really means.

Some ideas are related by **sequence**, or time order. Example A asks what happened right after the bus left the school. To answer this question, you have to read the four choices and decide in what order they occurred. The correct answer is Ⓓ, *The group began throwing things*. This event is stated in the first paragraph. Choices Ⓐ and Ⓑ happen later in the story, and choice Ⓒ does not happen in this passage at all.

Some passages **compare and contrast** two or more ideas by suggesting how they are alike and how they are different. Example B asks how Mara and Sandy are different. From the different ways the girls respond to the teasing, it is clear that the correct answer is Ⓒ, *Sandy is bolder than Mara*. Mara blushes and feels embarrassed, but Sandy responds by teasing right back.

Some ideas are related by **cause and effect**. Example C asks why the other students don't report the gang to the bus driver. The reason is because *they are afraid of the group*, choice Ⓑ. This reason is implied, or suggested, in the first paragraph.

Example D is also about cause and effect. Mara blushed at Sam's teasing because she *felt self-conscious*, choice Ⓐ. You know this is the reason because she feels embarrassed about the shape of her head and the jumpsuit she is wearing. There is no evidence to suggest that any of the other choices is true.

Test-Taking Tips

1 Be careful when looking for the sequence of events. The events are not always described in the order in which they occur.

2 When you want to find the sequence of events, look for signal words such as *first, then, next, before, just as, finally, last,* and *after* (as in "The bus had *just* left the school...").

3 When you want to find causes and effects, look for signal words and phrases such as *because, as a result, the reason why, since, so, as a consequence, thus,* and *therefore*. (For example: "Sam was the worst, *because* all of his insults...".)

4 When you compare two or more things, look for signal words such as *like, different, same, but, unlike, however,* and *on the other hand*.

Go for it

Test Practice 6: Constructing Meaning

Time: **8** minutes

Directions: Read the passage. Choose the best answer to each question.

Serenity stood in the line that snaked through the cafeteria and wondered why — no matter what was being served — the room always smelled like damp mashed potatoes. Somebody poked her in the back. "Hey, no cutting in line," yelled the tail of the snake.

"I'm not cutting," retorted Andy Garcia. "Serenity, can I ask you a few questions for the school newspaper while you eat?" Serenity nodded.

A few minutes later they were sitting at a table. Serenity was gobbling down a tunafish sandwich (she was starving) and looking forward to the split-pea soup. The vanilla pudding smelled good, but the skin on top looked thick enough to skate on.

Andy opened his bag lunch and took out three carrot sticks and a carton of yogurt. No wonder he was as skinny as the pencil tucked over his ear.

"Now, Serenity, there is a rumor going around that you're the prankster who changed the letters on the school sign last week."

Serenity just grinned and opened her carton of milk.

"Yes or no, Serenity?"

"I refuse to answer on the grounds that I might get into a whole lot of trouble," mumbled Serenity.

"What if I could assure you that everybody in the administration thinks it was pretty funny. Mr. Hassam told me that …" (Andy flipped through his notebook) " 'The kids need to let off steam once in a while. I don't mind as long as we get the missing letters back. They would cost money to replace.' "

"I never thought about that," mused Serenity.

"Just think of the headline." Andy used his carrot stick to write in the air. "SERENITY HAWKINS—CREATOR OF SCRAMBLED SIGN."

"Promise you won't mention my name," said Serenity, "and I'll let you know where the missing letters ended up."

"I promise," said Andy, exchanging his carrot for a real pencil.

Just then Bo Jenkins and some of his friends sat down at the table. "Too many curious people in here," said Serenity, scooping up the last spoonful of pudding. Then she stood up.

Outside, they sat on some dry, scratchy grass under an apple tree at the edge of the playground. A few ripe apples had fallen, and a sweet smell filled the air. The playground was full of people, but no one else was listening to Serenity.

"Where would you expect to find a letter for a sign?" asked Serenity.

For a minute Andy looked baffled. "On a sign?"

"Right. There's one taped to just about every sign in town."

"How many?" asked Andy excitedly.

"Let's see," Serenity counted on her fingers: BISHOP COUNTY JUNIOR HIGH SCHOOL has 28 letters, and BISHOP COUNTY JAIL only has 16 (I had to turn the U in JUNIOR upside down to make the A in JAIL). That leaves 12."

"The paper could sponsor a hunt. It would be great publicity."

"Fine," said Serenity, "as long as it's your publicity and not mine."

1. Which of these events occurred first?

   Ⓐ Andy approached Serenity in the cafeteria.

   Ⓑ Serenity put the letters all over town.

   Ⓒ Andy talked to members of the school administration.

   Ⓓ Serenity changed the message on the school sign.

2. What did Serenity do right after she finished her pudding?

   Ⓐ She ate her tunafish sandwich.

   Ⓑ She got back into the lunch line.

   Ⓒ She went outside.

   Ⓓ She borrowed a pencil from Andy.

3. Why did Serenity tell Andy where the missing letters were hidden?

   Ⓐ She realized that Mr. Hassam was angry with her.

   Ⓑ She realized that the letters were worth money.

   Ⓒ She wanted people to think Andy had scrambled the sign.

   Ⓓ She wanted everybody to know that she had taken the letters.

4. Andy cut into the lunch line because he wanted to —

   Ⓐ get some food

   Ⓑ warn Serenity that she was in trouble

   Ⓒ ask Serenity to help him organize a hunt

   Ⓓ get some information from Serenity

5. Because Bo Jenkins and his friends sat down, Serenity wanted to —

   Ⓐ leave the cafeteria

   Ⓑ play another trick

   Ⓒ eat more lunch

   Ⓓ keep the missing letters

6. How is the playground different from the cafeteria?

   Ⓐ The playground is noisier.

   Ⓑ The playground smells better.

   Ⓒ There are more people out on the playground.

   Ⓓ Everyone is listening to Serenity on the playground.

7. How are Andy and Serenity alike?

   Ⓐ Both are very determined.

   Ⓑ Both are wild and rebellious.

   Ⓒ Both love to play tricks on other people.

   Ⓓ Both love to eat a lot of food.

8. Serenity didn't want any publicity because —

   Ⓐ she was afraid she would get in trouble

   Ⓑ the other kids would make fun of her

   Ⓒ she was not the person who changed the sign

   Ⓓ everyone in school read the school newspaper

Number Correct/Total = _____ /8

31

Drawing Conclusions

Using logical reasoning to analyze a reading passage

Directions: Read the passage. Choose the best answer to each question.

Nine thousand years ago in a village in Syria, inhabitants carved designs into their limestone floors. In another ancient city in what is now Turkey, archaeologists have discovered a floor made of bright orange chips of stone embedded in cement. These two discoveries, and others like them, can tell us a lot about how the people of long ago built and decorated their homes.

In the city of Jericho in ancient Palestine, buildings were made with clay floors. The clay was then covered with plaster that had been tinted a red or cream color, and the plaster was brightly polished, creating a tough, shiny surface that has remained intact for thousands of years.

The inhabitants of Jericho also decorated the walls of their houses. They created geometric designs using red or cream-colored paints made from minerals, or black paint tinted with soot.

A The plaster used to cover the floors of Jericho was most likely tinted with —

Ⓐ minerals

Ⓑ cement

Ⓒ soot

Ⓓ lime

B Which generalization is supported by the information in this passage?

Ⓐ Geometric wall designs were a common feature of the homes in most ancient cities.

Ⓑ The inhabitants of ancient cities used various techniques to decorate their homes.

Ⓒ The Syrians were better builders than the Turks.

Ⓓ Ancient floors were planned to last for thousands of years.

Writers do not always state everything directly. They often imply, or suggest, information that you must figure out. The process of figuring out this information is called **drawing conclusions**. For example, if you read a description of a scene in which people are carrying umbrellas, and cars have their windshield wipers on, you can conclude, or infer, that it is raining.

To complete the sentence in Example A, you have to make a kind of conclusion called an **inference**. The passage does not state precisely what was used to tint the plaster on the floors in Jericho. However, the passage does state that the plaster was tinted a red or cream color, and it also states that the red and cream paints used on the walls were made using minerals. Therefore, it is reasonable to infer that the red and cream plaster mixtures were also tinted with *minerals*. Choice Ⓐ is correct.

In this kind of question, you would take two or more pieces of information and draw a specific conclusion or inference. You can set this up in a kind of formula, like this:

A. Plaster used on the floors was tinted a red or cream color.

+ B. Red and cream paints used on the walls were made with minerals.

= Therefore, the plaster was probably tinted with the same minerals.

Example B asks for a different kind of conclusion, called a **generalization**. This requires a different kind of reasoning based on the information you have read. To form a generalization, you must look at the specific pieces of information given. Then you can make a general statement that is based on these specific details.

The article describes several methods of building and decorating floors and walls that were used by people in ancient cities. So, the correct answer is Ⓑ. Choice Ⓐ is incorrect because geometric walls are only mentioned in one of the cities, Jericho. Choice Ⓒ is incorrect because there is no evidence that one type of building is better or worse than another. Choice Ⓓ is incorrect because, although some of the floors described have held up for thousands of years, there is no information to indicate that they were intended to last so long.

Test-Taking Tips

1 Make sure that the inference you choose makes sense, based on what you know from the passage.

2 Look back at the passage to find pieces of specific information that can help you draw a conclusion.

3 When you are looking for a generalization, look for a general statement that holds true for all of the specific examples in the passage. Watch out for absolute words in the answer choices, such as *all*, *none*, and *every*. The statement "Most people like ice cream" is much more likely to be true than the statement "Everyone likes ice cream."

4 Make sure that the generalization you choose can be supported by the information in the passage. If you find one example that does not support the generalization, it is probably wrong.

Go for it

Test Practice 7 : Drawing Conclusions   Time: 8 minutes

Directions: Read the passage. Choose the best answer to each question.

For nearly thirty years, the British-born scientist Jane Goodall has lived and worked in Tanzania, Africa. Her home is Gombe National Park, and her work is studying the wild chimpanzees that live there, protected from the hunters and other dangers that face chimpanzees elsewhere in Africa.

One typical morning, Jane rises early and climbs up into the hills, looking for a group of chimpanzees. She spots twenty-year-old Gremlin holding her sleeping baby, Galahad. Jane takes out her notebook and begins to write her observations. She will follow this pair until dusk.

Accompanying Galahad and Gremlin are Gremlin's two brothers, Goblin and Gimble. Another adult male suddenly appears, and Goblin charges toward him — stamping, leaping, and threatening. More chimps appear and the air is filled with screams as the animals wrestle and pound each other. Suddenly, the chimpanzees calm down. One of the newcomers crouches in front of Goblin, and Goblin touches him gently. At this signal, the two groups of chimps begin to embrace and then to groom each other, combing and cleaning their fur. This process lasts for an hour. Then Goblin leads his family into the forest.

Finding a fig tree, Gremlin climbs it, carrying her baby with her. He sits beside her, watching as his mother eats figs for an hour. The baby touches the figs but does not eat them. He has only four teeth and still depends upon his mother's milk for nutrition.

After descending the tree, Gremlin encounters three more chimps: Fifi, Flossi, and Fanni. Gremlin sits down to rest, and Flossi and Fanni begin to play, nibbling and tickling each other and making a noise that sounds like laughter. Baby Galahad watches; soon he will play with other young chimps. When the game is over, Fanni steals bananas from Jane's pocket.

Flossi, Fanni, and Fifi climb into a tree and begin to eat leaves. Jane Goodall notices Frodo, another of Fifi's chidren, in a nearby palm tree. He is chewing on palm fronds and sucking out the juice.

It is now late afternoon. Jane loses sight of Gremlin and Galahad, but encounters two more chimpanzees. They are the nine-year-old female Wunda and her little brother Wolfi. Their mother has died recently, and Wunda has her arms around her little brother. This sight reassures Jane. In the past she has known baby chimpanzees who were so upset by the deaths of their mothers that they themselves fell ill and died — even though other chimps were feeding them. Wunda climbs a tree for some food. When little Wolfi cries, she reaches back and helps him up.

On the ground nearby is Wunda's older brother, Wilkie. He is pushing a piece of grass into a termite nest. Then he pulls the grass out and eats the termites that are clinging to it. On other occasions, Jane Goodall has seen chimps use sticks to "fish" for ants.

The sun is setting. Goodall returns to her house beside Lake Tanganyika. Tomorrow she will follow the chimpanzees again.

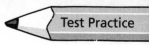

1. Which generalization is best supported by the information in this passage?

   Ⓐ Baby chimpanzees are very dependent upon their mothers.

   Ⓑ Male chimpanzees are usually gentle and passive.

   Ⓒ Chimpanzees spend most of the time grooming themselves.

   Ⓓ Most African chimpanzees live in protected parks.

2. Based on the information in this passage, you can conclude that chimpanzees are very —

   Ⓐ violent

   Ⓑ lazy

   Ⓒ social

   Ⓓ unintelligent

3. Adult Gombe chimpanzees get most of their food from —

   Ⓐ Jane Goodall

   Ⓑ trees

   Ⓒ underground

   Ⓓ their mothers

4. Galahad will most likely begin to eat figs when —

   Ⓐ his mother has another baby

   Ⓑ the figs get riper

   Ⓒ he learns to climb better

   Ⓓ he gets more teeth

5. Goodall names chimps in the same family with names that —

   Ⓐ begin with the same letter

   Ⓑ come from fairy tales

   Ⓒ rhyme with each other

   Ⓓ describe each chimp's "personality"

6. When other chimpanzees enter Goblin's territory, his behavior toward them is most likely intended to —

   Ⓐ show that he is boss

   Ⓑ ask for their help

   Ⓒ drive them away

   Ⓓ obtain food from them

7. What inference can be drawn from the behavior of chimps whose mothers have died?

   Ⓐ Chimpanzees cannot remember individuals or events from the past.

   Ⓑ Chimpanzees have emotional as well as physical needs.

   Ⓒ Adult chimpanzees will only care for their own babies.

   Ⓓ Orphan chimps cannot get along with other chimps.

8. What generalization can be made from Wilkie's "fishing" for termites and other chimps "fishing" for ants?

   Ⓐ Chimpanzees prefer eating insects to fruits.

   Ⓑ Chimpanzees can build complex objects.

   Ⓒ Chimpanzees have very good vision.

   Ⓓ Chimpanzees can use objects as tools.

Number Correct/Total = _____ /8

Evaluating Information

Making judgments about what you read

Directions: Read the passage. Choose the best answer to each question.

I was walking down the street with my friend Elmo, when Elmo said to me, "You know, Shanta, you should really learn how to board."

"Forget it," I answered. "I'd kill myself if I got on a skateboard."

Just then Buzz and Bo, the Dreiser twins, came whizzing down the sidewalk and nearly flattened us.

"If Bo Dreiser can do it, so can you," said Elmo. "You just need a good teacher." He took the skateboard he'd been carrying and placed it on the pavement in front of me. "Just stand on it for one second; you can hold onto my arm for balance."

I carefully placed my left foot on the board. So far, so good. I followed with my right. Immediately I had the sensation of standing on the deck of a small boat in a big storm. The board swung sideways and I flipped into the air, turned one-and-a-quarter times, and landed neatly on one knee, producing a scrape roughly the shape and size of Australia.

Elmo stared at me in disbelief. "That was totally awesome," he said. "A little more practice and you could compete."

A In this passage, the author's purpose is to —

Ⓐ give information about skateboards

Ⓑ persuade people to buy skateboards

Ⓒ compare skateboards with bicycles

Ⓓ entertain with a story about skateboarding

B Which statement from the story is an opinion?

Ⓐ I was walking down the street with my friend Elmo.

Ⓑ Just then the Dreiser twins came buzzing down the sidewalk.

Ⓒ "If Bo Dreiser can do it, so can you."

Ⓓ I followed with my right.

C The narrator most likely feels that skateboards are —

Ⓐ lots of fun

Ⓑ dangerous toys

Ⓒ dull and boring

Ⓓ useful tools

D Which statement is most likely an exaggeration?

Ⓐ I carefully placed my left foot on the board.

Ⓑ The board swung sideways and I flipped into the air.

Ⓒ The scrape was roughly the size of Australia.

Ⓓ Elmo stared in disbelief.

36   Reading Comprehension Unit

To answer these kinds of questions, you have to think about what you read and make judgments. This is called **evaluating information**.

Some questions may ask what the author thinks or why the author wrote the passage. What the author thinks is the **author's point of view** toward, or opinion on, the subject, negative or positive. Why the author wrote the passage is the **author's purpose**. Most stories are written to entertain or to teach a lesson. Advertisements are written to persuade. In informational texts, the author's purpose is to give information or describe something.

Example A asks about the author's purpose. Why did the author write this passage? The correct answer is Ⓓ, *to entertain with a story about skateboarding*. The other choices are incorrect because the author doesn't give much information about skateboards, Ⓐ, does give one reason *not* to buy skateboards, Ⓑ, and doesn't even mention bicycles, Ⓒ.

Example C asks about the author's opinion of skateboards. Based on what happens to Shanta, the story suggests that the author thinks skateboards are *dangerous*, choice Ⓑ.

Other questions may ask you to distinguish between facts and opinions in what you read. A **fact** is something that can be proven true. An **opinion** is a feeling or belief. In Example B, three of the choices are facts that can be proven true. The correct answer, Ⓒ, is an opinion stated by Elmo.

Some questions may ask you to use the information in the passage to **make judgments** or decisions. Test questions may ask you to make a variety of different kinds of judgments: to decide whether a statement is true or false, to choose the best reason for doing something, to judge the quality of some part of the story itself, and so on.

Example D asks you to make a judgment about statements from the passage. Common sense suggests that the correct answer is Ⓒ. Shanta exaggerates about the scrape on her knee. The other choices all describe things that probably happened just the way they say.

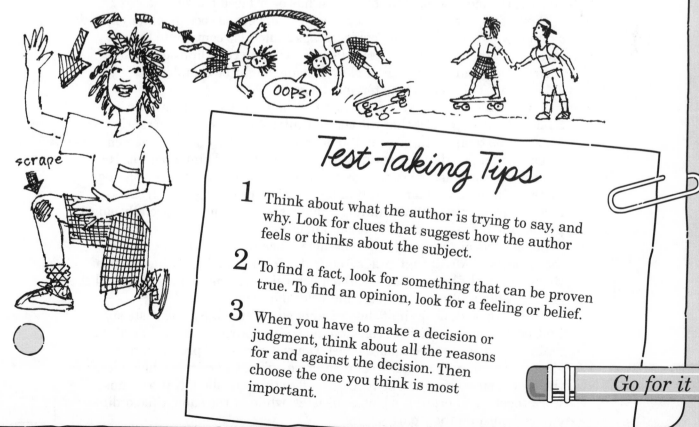

scrape

OOPS!

Test-Taking Tips

1 Think about what the author is trying to say, and why. Look for clues that suggest how the author feels or thinks about the subject.

2 To find a fact, look for something that can be proven true. To find an opinion, look for a feeling or belief.

3 When you have to make a decision or judgment, think about all the reasons for and against the decision. Then choose the one you think is most important.

Go for it

Test Practice 8: Evaluating Information

Time: **8** minutes

Directions: Read the passage. Choose the best answer to each question.

The "greenhouse effect" is a term used to describe the warming of the earth due to increasing amounts of carbon dioxide in the atmosphere. Carbon dioxide is a gas that is produced every time a fuel such as coal, oil, or natural gas is burned. This carbon dioxide increases the heat of the atmosphere, and thus warms the planet.

According to some scientists, the greenhouse effect is imaginary. Others say it may even be beneficial. These people are wrong. The greenhouse effect is the most serious problem that has ever faced our planet.

First of all, the level of the ocean could rise, because ocean water expands as it grows warmer. Melting polar icecaps could also contribute to an increase in the level of the ocean. People living on coastlines might lose their homes, and cities such as New Orleans might be completely submerged. This would be a terrible tragedy!

Parts of the world that are already hot might become unbearably so. Some scientists predict that the city of Dallas, Texas, which currently experiences temperatures over 100 degrees Fahrenheit about nineteen days a year, might get that hot seventy-eight days a year! Think about it. Hot weather doesn't just mean that people feel a little yucky. It means a huge increase in the use of air conditioning (which uses energy, which costs money, and creates pollution). It can make some people — especially elderly people and infants — very ill. It can kill crops.

Some parts of the world might become much drier. There are already many parts of Africa that suffer frequently from droughts. Other parts of the world might become wetter. Too much rain in some regions could kill the crops traditionally grown there, and lead to hunger.

What can be done to limit the greenhouse effect? Many scientists suggest that people need to learn to conserve fuel, since burning fuel is one of the main causes of the greenhouse effect. Governments can protect forests, since trees can help reduce the greenhouse effect. Chemicals which increase the greenhouse effect can be banned or strictly controlled. Nations must work together to prevent a global disaster, while at the same time ordinary citizens must do their part.

1. In this passage, the author's purpose is to —

   Ⓐ persuade people that there is no greenhouse effect
   Ⓑ tell a terrifying story about the greenhouse effect
   Ⓒ inform people about the greenhouse effect
   Ⓓ explain why the greenhouse effect cannot be prevented

2. The author of this passage most likely thinks that the greenhouse effect is —

   Ⓐ an imaginary problem
   Ⓑ a serious threat
   Ⓒ a beneficial process
   Ⓓ a temporary discomfort

3. Which statement from the passage is a fact?

   Ⓐ These people are wrong.
   Ⓑ The greenhouse effect is the most serious problem that has ever faced our planet.
   Ⓒ This would be a terrible tragedy!
   Ⓓ It can make some people — especially elderly people and infants — very ill.

4. Which sentence uses language that is inappropriate to the rest of the passage?

   Ⓐ Melting polar icecaps could contribute to an increase in the level of the ocean.
   Ⓑ This doesn't just mean a little yucky weather.
   Ⓒ Other parts of the world might become wetter.
   Ⓓ Governments can protect forests, since trees can help reduce the greenhouse effect.

5. Which statement from the passage is an opinion?

   Ⓐ Hot weather means a huge increase in air conditioning.
   Ⓑ Many parts of Africa already suffer from droughts.
   Ⓒ Ordinary citizens must do their part.
   Ⓓ Carbon dioxide is a gas produced when a fuel such as coal or oil is burned.

6. Ordinary citizens can best help reduce the greenhouse effect by —

   Ⓐ conserving fuel
   Ⓑ using more air conditioning
   Ⓒ banning certain chemicals
   Ⓓ burning more natural gas

7. What would be the most serious problem caused by the greenhouse effect?

   Ⓐ Houses would be lost.
   Ⓑ People would die from hunger.
   Ⓒ Infants would become ill.
   Ⓓ The weather would become quite uncomfortable.

8. The author of this passage seems to think that this problem can best be solved by —

   Ⓐ ordinary citizens
   Ⓑ the U.S. government
   Ⓒ factory owners
   Ⓓ nations working together

Number Correct/Total = _____ /8

Characters and Plot

Understanding the characters and plot in a story

Directions: Read the passage. Choose the best answer to each question.

Lita stood in line for the merry-go-round for the tenth time. Some of her friends went by on their way to the bumper cars.

"Aren't you bored yet, Lita?"

"No!" yelled Lita with a huge smile. "I just love the merry-go-round! I even have a favorite horse!"

But when she climbed up on the yellow horse for the tenth time, her smile disappeared. There was nobody watching; her friends were all on the more exciting rides: the Sky Diver, the roller coaster, the bumper cars, and the double Ferris wheel. She was on the merry-go-round with a bunch of six-year-olds. She wanted to be with her friends, but she kept imagining the Ferris wheel tipping over or the car shooting off the roller coaster. She hated her stupid imagination.

When the merry-go-round stopped turning, she got off slowly. Somebody grabbed her elbow. It was Lily King. "Come on now, Lita!" she urged. "We're going to throw balls at a target. If we hit it, Nicki's big brother gets dunked in a pool of cold water."

Lita grinned again, and this time her smile was for real.

A How does Lita feel when she gets on the merry-go-round for the tenth time?

 Ⓐ sad

 Ⓑ excited

 Ⓒ terrified

 Ⓓ proud

B Why doesn't Lita go on any of the other rides?

 Ⓐ Her friends are ignoring her.

 Ⓑ She is afraid.

 Ⓒ She enjoys going on the merry-go-round.

 Ⓓ The other rides are too crowded.

C At the end of the story, Lily King wants to —

 Ⓐ go to a food stand

 Ⓑ ride the bumper cars

 Ⓒ ride the roller coaster

 Ⓓ play a game

D What will Lita most likely do next?

 Ⓐ go on the roller coaster

 Ⓑ ride the merry-go-round again

 Ⓒ go for a swim

 Ⓓ go with Lily and the others

HEY!

This kind of story usually has two kinds of questions. One kind of question asks about the **characters** — the people, or sometimes animals — in the story. The other kind of question is about the **plot**, or events that happen in the story.

Questions about the characters may ask how a character feels about something, what kind of person the character is, or why a character does something in the story. They may also ask you to find clues that tell you about the character, and how you know she is honest, or sad, etc.

Example A asks how Lita feels when she gets on the merry-go-round again. Since the story states that Lita's smile disappears when there is nobody watching her, and she clearly wishes she could be with her friends, the correct answer is Ⓐ, *sad*.

Example B tests your understanding of a character's motives, or why a character does something. Lita imagines terrible accidents that will happen if she goes on the Ferris wheel or the roller coaster, so she doesn't go on those rides. She is afraid. Choice Ⓑ is correct.

Questions about the plot ask about events in the story. They may also ask you to predict what will happen next, based on what has happened so far.

Example C asks what Lily King wants to do at the end of the story. She says, "We're going to throw balls at a target." So the correct answer is Ⓓ, she wants to *play a game*.

Example D asks you to predict what will happen next. You know from the rest of the story that Lita is tired of the merry-go-round, so choice Ⓑ is incorrect. You know she wants to be with her friends. When Lily King invites her to go play a game, she will most likely go with her, so the answer is Ⓓ. She is afraid of the roller coaster, so choice Ⓐ is not likely, and swimming has not been mentioned at all, so Ⓒ is incorrect.

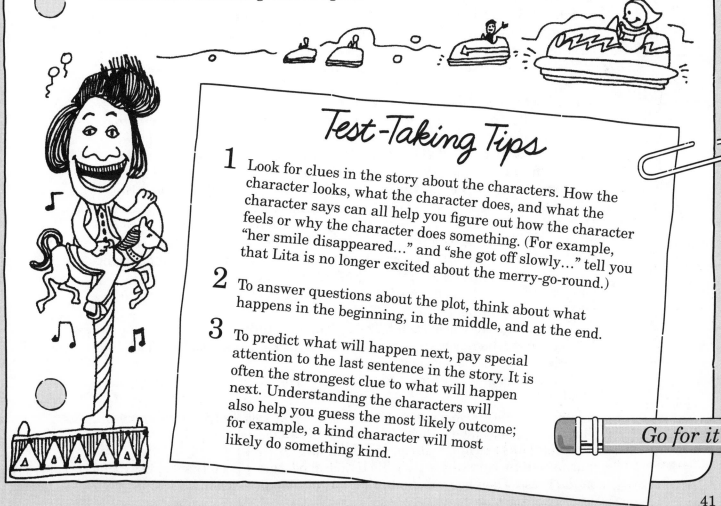

Test-Taking Tips

1 Look for clues in the story about the characters. How the character looks, what the character does, and what the character says can all help you figure out how the character feels or why the character does something. (For example, "her smile disappeared..." and "she got off slowly..." tell you that Lita is no longer excited about the merry-go-round.)

2 To answer questions about the plot, think about what happens in the beginning, in the middle, and at the end.

3 To predict what will happen next, pay special attention to the last sentence in the story. It is often the strongest clue to what will happen next. Understanding the characters will also help you guess the most likely outcome; for example, a kind character will most likely do something kind.

Go for it

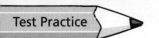

Test Practice 9: Characters and Plot

Time: **8** minutes

Directions: Read the passage. Choose the best answer to each question.

Chad sat in the front of the canoe, frowning. His arms and shoulders ached from paddling for so long, but he could put up with that. What he couldn't stand was Uncle David's constant criticism from the back of the canoe.

"Don't work so hard, Chad." "Watch how I handle the paddle, Chad." "Try not to make a sound, Chad." "You're getting yourself exhausted for no reason, Chad."

It was Chad's first time in a canoe. When Uncle David had asked if he wanted to take the short route or the long one, he yelled out, "Oh, the long one of course!" That was this morning, when the river was still nice and cool.

He had jumped into the canoe and Uncle David had yelled, "Careful — you'll put a foot through!"

Embarrassed, Chad had tried to paddle extra hard, to impress his uncle. But it turned out if you really knew what to do in a canoe, you didn't have to paddle hard. Five hours after their departure, Chad was soaked in sweat and his hands were covered with blisters. Uncle David looked as cool as a cucumber, except for his nose, which was turning bright red.

"Darn," muttered Uncle David about once every ten minutes, "I wish I'd brought that sunscreen. Darn."

Finally he suggested that they stop and open their picnic basket. He spotted a little creek running into the river, and he steered the canoe into it. The creek meandered through a meadow. They paddled quietly until they found a smooth, grassy bank. They pulled the canoe ashore and ate their lunch. Uncle David smiled and sighed with pleasure as he devoured turkey and tomato sandwiches and guzzled iced tea. Chad frowned as he ate. He felt a little better, but he couldn't think of anything to say. He didn't want Uncle David to think he was sulking like a baby. Chad leaped into the water to cool off. The bed of the stream felt unusually smooth and firm underfoot. He reached down to see what it was made of and brought up a handful of bright blue clay. Quickly he daubed the clay all over his face, neck and shoulders. Grabbing a handful of long reeds he turned and charged toward his uncle, making loud, inhuman sounds.

"Whoa!" laughed Uncle David. Then he made a face.

"Goodness, Chad, how can you stand that muck all over you? You look like something out of a horror movie."

"The Swamp Monster meets Rudolph the Red-Nosed Reindeer," laughed Chad.

Uncle David rubbed his nose ruefully. "It hurts, too. If only I hadn't left that sunscreen at home. Darn. I should have put on a nice thick coat of sunscreen this morning." He looked thoughtfully at Chad. "Hey …" he murmured. He carefully untied his tennis shoes and placed them side by side on the grass. Then he waded into the stream. Bending down, he scooped up a handful of the blue clay.

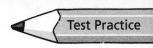

1. How does Chad feel about his decision to take the long route down the river?

   Ⓐ proud

   Ⓑ ashamed

   Ⓒ relieved

   Ⓓ regretful

2. What kind of person is Chad?

   Ⓐ slow and cautious

   Ⓑ eager and thoughtless

   Ⓒ bitter and unforgiving

   Ⓓ shy and serious

3. Why does Chad cover himself with clay?

   Ⓐ He is angry with his uncle and wants to frighten him.

   Ⓑ He wants to conceal himself from his uncle.

   Ⓒ He wants to find a way to make up with his uncle.

   Ⓓ He wants to soothe his sunburned skin.

4. What kind of person is Uncle David?

   Ⓐ tactful and charming

   Ⓑ vague and impractical

   Ⓒ wild and unpredictable

   Ⓓ careful and serious

5. Chad and his uncle paddle up the stream in order to —

   Ⓐ find a place to eat lunch

   Ⓑ go swimming

   Ⓒ shorten their trip

   Ⓓ find some blue clay

6. How does Uncle David feel when he sees Chad all covered with blue clay?

   Ⓐ surprised and frightened

   Ⓑ amused but disgusted

   Ⓒ envious but proud

   Ⓓ irritated and bored

7. What is wrong with Uncle David's nose?

   Ⓐ It is getting sunburned.

   Ⓑ He bumped it with one of the paddles.

   Ⓒ He has a bad cold.

   Ⓓ He hurt it while swimming.

8. Chad paddled extra hard in the morning because he wanted to —

   Ⓐ get a lot of exercise

   Ⓑ stay cool in the breeze

   Ⓒ get home as quickly as possible

   Ⓓ make his uncle think he was a good canoeist

9. Uncle David was upset all day because he —

   Ⓐ didn't like Chad

   Ⓑ forgot his sunscreen

   Ⓒ was hot and tired

   Ⓓ had blisters on his hands

10. What will Uncle David probably do next?

    Ⓐ ask Chad to paddle by himself

    Ⓑ put some clay on his nose

    Ⓒ punish Chad for scaring him

    Ⓓ rest in the shade

Number Correct/Total = _____ /10

Reading Literature

Recognizing types of literature and their characteristics

Directions: Read the passage. Choose the best answer to each question.

It was a dark and windy night. Thin clouds blew across the sky like bits of tattered gray silk. The moon was a razor's edge of white. The orphan girl, Jessica, toiled up the steep side of the mountain, clutching her thin cloak and shivering. She stared ahead to the towers that rose black against the sky, willing herself to continue. Suddenly, her vision blurred, and she sank exhausted to the stony path.

She had nearly fainted, but some small spark of consciousness remained alight. "I must get up," she thought, "or I will die of cold and hunger. I've got to get to the castle."

But her legs felt as if they were made of lead, she was dizzy, and her hands trembled. She had gone without food for two days.

A dangerous thought entered her mind. "I'd probably feel better if I lay down and slept for a while. It's really not so cold." In fact, she was beginning to grow numb. She closed her eyes and laid her head down on the hard earth as if it were a pillow.

Suddenly there was a loud cry just above her head. Terrified, she jumped to her feet. An owl glared down at her from the gnarled branches of an oak and screeched urgently again.

Realizing she had nearly fallen asleep, Jessica forced herself up the hill. Half an hour later, she was seated in the kitchen of the castle, eating a bowl of hot soup that the cook had given her.

A "Thin clouds blew across the sky like bits of tattered gray silk" means that —

    Ⓐ The clouds looked ragged and gray.

    Ⓑ The clouds were made of cloth.

    Ⓒ Bits of fabric were floating in the air.

    Ⓓ The wind was tearing Jessica's silk cloak.

B What is the mood of this story?

    Ⓐ playful

    Ⓑ peaceful

    Ⓒ humorous

    Ⓓ suspenseful

C What is the climax of this story?

    Ⓐ Jessica sinks exhausted to the stony ground.

    Ⓑ Jessica falls asleep.

    Ⓒ The owl wakes up Jessica.

    Ⓓ The cook serves Jessica a bowl of hot soup.

D This story is told by —

    Ⓐ an orphan girl named Jessica

    Ⓑ the cook at the castle

    Ⓒ the owl that screeches

    Ⓓ an outside observer

These kinds of questions are about **reading literature**: the setting and structure of the story, narrative point of view, language used by the author, and recognizing different kinds of literature.

Some questions ask about language used in a story. Writers use different kinds of language to make their writing more interesting. The sentence in Example A is an example of **figurative language**: language that suggests something other than what the words actually mean. This example is a figure of speech called a *simile*, in which the writer compares the clouds to "bits of tattered gray silk." This actually means that the clouds were *ragged and gray*, choice Ⓐ. It does not mean that pieces of silk cloth were blowing across the sky.

Some questions ask about the theme or mood of the story. The **theme** is the message or the lesson that the writer is trying to express. The **mood** is the feeling you get from the story. Example B asks for the mood. The writer's descriptions of the dark night, the wind, and Jessica's life-and-death situation make the story *suspenseful*, so Ⓓ is correct.

Some questions ask about the **setting** of the story, where and when the story takes place, or its **structure**. Most

stories like this have a certain structure. It begins with a *problem*, or conflict. Then it builds to a *climax*, or high point. Then it slowly winds down again as the character solves the problem or resolves the conflict.

In this story, Jessica has a problem: she has to reach the castle before something terrible happens to her. The story builds to the climax, which occurs when the owl screeches and wakes up Jessica. Example C asks for the climax of the story; the answer is Ⓒ. Then Jessica solves her problem by reaching the castle at the end.

Every story is told by a character in the story or an outside observer, called a *third-person narrator*. The storyteller's perspective is the **narrative point of view**. Example D asks about who is telling this story. Since the narrator follows Jessica all the way through and refers to her as *she,* the narrator must be an *outside observer*, choice Ⓓ. If Jessica were telling the story, she would say "*I toiled up the steep side of the mountain…*".

Some reading tests also ask questions about **genres**, or kinds, of literature. Kinds of literature usually include historical fiction, realistic fiction, science fiction, fantasy, myth, folk tales, and mystery.

Test-Taking Tips

1 The language that a writer uses in a piece of literature is very important, especially in poetry. Watch for phrases that suggest something different from what the words actually say.

2 Look for details that tell you when and where the story takes place, and what events happen in the story.

3 To find the narrative point of view, look for clue words, such as *I, me, he, she,* and *they*. A first-person narrator is usually a character in the story; a third-person narrator is usually an outside observer.

Go for it

Test Practice 10 : Reading Literature

Time: **10** minutes

Directions: Read the passage. Choose the best answer to each question.

April 3. The kittens were born last night. So far, all four have survived. The children are determined to find out where I have hidden them. They stand guard beside me when I come inside to eat, and then try to follow me when I go back outside. But I am too quick and clever for them, and they haven't discovered my hiding place under the shed. I'll show them the kittens when I'm good and ready.

April 10. I carried three of the kittens into the Big House today, one by one, gently holding them in my mouth. Everyone cooed over how cute they are. But the cutest of all, the little ginger-colored one with the big ears, is still under the shed. Every year they take all my kittens away from me, but this year I'll outwit them.

April 15. I had a close call today. The Boy was out kicking his soccer ball around the yard and smacked it into the side of the shed by mistake. It must have sounded like the end of the world to Ginger, for she set to meowing. Her cries pierced the quiet air like needles. The Boy listened and started toward the shed. In a panic, I darted up a nearby tree and made a lot of noise, pretending to be after a nest. He looked up at me and scolded, "Now, Dot, you leave those birds alone." It worked.

May 1. The kittens are getting bigger. The three in the Big House stagger around and play in the kitchen, their little claws catching in the big hooked rug. They get lots of attention from the Boy and the Girl, and even the Mother once in a while. I sneak out as often as possible to play with Ginger and feed her. She's starting to get more adventurous, and I'm afraid she'll come prowling up into the yard when one of Them is around.

May 9. The Mother said it's almost time to find homes for the kittens. The Boy brought over a friend who claimed the striped one. The Girl said some of her friends are interested.

May 15. Well, Stripey, Black Paws, and Gray Whiskers are all gone. I looked carefully at each of their new parents, and luckily they met with my approval. If they hadn't, there would have been some scratched ankles in the Big House. Now I can spend all my time with Ginger until I judge the right moment has come.

May 16. The Girl is sad. She says she misses the kittens.

May 17. Heard the Boy complaining today. He asked why they couldn't keep just one. I almost brought Ginger up then, but got nervous. I have to be sure!

May 18. Heard the Mother talking to the Father today. She says the children want two cats, and she agrees! The time has come!

May 19. I brought Ginger up to the Big House this morning. They were all sitting around the breakfast table when in she sauntered, tail up, head high. What a beautiful baby she is! They loved her! "Why, Dot," they exclaimed, "how did you manage to hide this one? Clever Dot." "Can we keep her?" asked the Boy. "I don't see why not," answered the Father. Ginger and I shared a bowl of milk and then a nap in the sunny corner.

GO ON

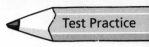

1. The major conflict in this story is between the—

   Ⓐ mother cat and her kittens

   Ⓑ human children and their parents

   Ⓒ mother cat and the humans

   Ⓓ Ginger and the other three kittens

2. This story is written in the form of a —

   Ⓐ letter

   Ⓑ scientific report

   Ⓒ magazine article

   Ⓓ diary

3. This story is told by —

   Ⓐ Dot

   Ⓑ Ginger

   Ⓒ the Mother

   Ⓓ the Girl

4. What type of story is this?

   Ⓐ mystery

   Ⓑ animal story

   Ⓒ science fiction

   Ⓓ folk tale

5. "Her cries pierced the quiet air like needles" means that —

   Ⓐ Her sharp cries created a loud disturbance.

   Ⓑ She cried out loud when she was pricked with needles.

   Ⓒ Her cries made tiny holes in the air around her.

   Ⓓ She thought she had been pricked by a needle.

6. This story takes place at a —

   Ⓐ veterinarian's office

   Ⓑ large farm

   Ⓒ family home

   Ⓓ zoo

7. The climax of this story occurs when —

   Ⓐ Dot brings the first three kittens into the Big House.

   Ⓑ Dot hears the Mother say the family is ready for two cats.

   Ⓒ Dot hears the Boy complaining about the kittens being gone.

   Ⓓ Dot and Ginger share a bowl of milk in the Big House.

8. What is the mood of the story up until the climax?

   Ⓐ anxious

   Ⓑ joyous

   Ⓒ melancholy

   Ⓓ silly

9. At the end of the story, the family decides to —

   Ⓐ give Dot and Ginger away

   Ⓑ get all the kittens back

   Ⓒ keep Ginger as a second cat

   Ⓓ try to find a new cat

10. What is the theme of this story?

    Ⓐ It is best to accept things as they are.

    Ⓑ It is always best to be open and completely honest about what you are doing.

    Ⓒ It is wrong for people to have animals as pets.

    Ⓓ If you plan ahead and work hard, you can often find a way to reach your goals.

Number Correct/Total = _____ /10

This test will tell you how well you might score on a standardized reading test after using this book. If you compare your scores on Tryout Tests 1 and 2, you'll see how much you've learned!

Reading Tryout Test 2

Time: **30** minutes

Directions: Follow the directions for each part of the test. Read each question carefully and fill in the circle beside the answer you choose. The answer to the sample question (**S**) has been filled in for you.

Questions 1–3. Choose the meaning of the underlined word.

S a <u>congenial</u> attitude

Ⓐ unpleasant   ● agreeable

Ⓑ popular   Ⓓ mysterious

1. an old <u>brooch</u>
   Ⓐ small boat   Ⓒ decorative pin
   Ⓑ carriage   Ⓓ illustration

2. <u>enhance</u> the flavor
   Ⓐ improve   Ⓒ destroy
   Ⓑ disguise   Ⓓ enjoy

3. a <u>monotonous</u> job
   Ⓐ well-paying   Ⓒ complicated
   Ⓑ without variety   Ⓓ perfectly done

Questions 4–5. Fill in the circle next to the definition of the key word.

4. postgraduation
   Ⓐ against graduation
   Ⓑ before graduation
   Ⓒ without graduation
   Ⓓ after graduation

5. martyrdom
   Ⓐ able to be a martyr
   Ⓑ filled with martyrs
   Ⓒ state of being a martyr
   Ⓓ opposed to martyrs

Questions 6–8. Choose the best answer to each question.

6. Which word most likely comes from the French word *diapre*, meaning "cloth"?
   Ⓐ diamond   Ⓒ diary
   Ⓑ dipper   Ⓓ diaper

7. Which word most likely comes from the Latin word *spectare*, meaning "to behold"?
   Ⓐ special   Ⓒ spectator
   Ⓑ speaker   Ⓓ sparkler

8. Which word most likely comes from the Persian word *qand*, meaning "sugar"?
   Ⓐ candy   Ⓒ queen
   Ⓑ kind   Ⓓ sand

Questions 9–11. Choose the word that means the OPPOSITE of the key word.

9. methodical
   Ⓐ intelligent   Ⓒ fearful
   Ⓑ careless   Ⓓ generous

10. rejoice
    Ⓐ continue   Ⓒ cheer
    Ⓑ delay   Ⓓ grieve

11. tarnish
    Ⓐ punish   Ⓒ polish
    Ⓑ repay   Ⓓ embrace

GO ON

Questions 12–15. Choose the word that best fits the blank in the sentence.

12. We watched a _____ movie about a man who turns into a giraffe.

    Ⓐ solid   Ⓒ bizarre

    Ⓑ patient   Ⓓ benign

13. A red _____ flapped in the breeze.

    Ⓐ pennant   Ⓒ mast

    Ⓑ beauty   Ⓓ monument

14. A bystander saw the _____ steal the lady's purse.

    Ⓐ witness   Ⓒ performer

    Ⓑ culprit   Ⓓ artisan

15. Several boats were destroyed when the hurricane hit the _____.

    Ⓐ manger   Ⓒ vehicle

    Ⓑ esteem   Ⓓ marina

Questions 16–19. Choose the meaning of the underlined word in each sentence.

16. Jake acted like a buffoon at the party. He wore a pair of shorts on his head and made all sorts of monkey noises.

    Ⓐ guest   Ⓒ fool

    Ⓑ enemy   Ⓓ zookeeper

17. The movie star wore ostentatious jewelry such as huge diamond rings and thick gold necklaces.

    Ⓐ cheap   Ⓒ delicate

    Ⓑ old   Ⓓ showy

18. Three zealous environmentalists hugged the trees to save them from the loggers' saws.

    Ⓐ timid   Ⓒ devoted

    Ⓑ envious   Ⓓ affectionate

19. The stone ricocheted off the garage and broke the windshield of a car parked in the driveway.

    Ⓐ fell   Ⓒ rose

    Ⓑ bounced   Ⓓ slid

Questions 20–21. Look at the sentence in the box. Then choose the sentence below in which the underlined word is used in the same way.

20. | Mom walked around the block. |

    Ⓐ Merle leaped up to block the field goal attempt.

    Ⓑ The child added a block to the tower.

    Ⓒ I had a sudden mental block and could not remember her name.

    Ⓓ Go to the end of the block and turn right.

21. | The ring slipped off my finger. |

    Ⓐ Mel picked up the telephone after the second ring.

    Ⓑ The dancers formed a ring.

    Ⓒ His wedding ring was made of gold and diamonds.

    Ⓓ Police broke up the ring of smugglers.

GO ON

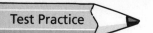

Reading Tryout Test 2 (continued)

Questions 22–35. Read each passage. Choose the best answer to each question.

An early English castle was not particularly comfortable. The castle's main function was to provide security from enemy attack. It was a simple structure: a tall wooden tower built on a hill and surrounded by a moat. Inside the tower were a storeroom, a hall, and a single bedroom called the *solar*.

The castle was inhabited by a lord and his family, a few soldiers, and some servants (except in time of war, when many who were loyal to the lord gathered in the tower to fight the enemy or seek protection).

The hall was the living and dining area. There was little privacy, and no luxury. Only the lord and his family had a permanent table; everyone else ate at trestle tables that could be taken apart and stacked between meals. And only the lord had a chair with a back! Everyone else — even the lord's poor wife — had to make do with a stool!

The lord sometimes owned valuable rings, and his wife wore bracelets. There might even have been a colorful tapestry hanging on the wall behind them. But they had few other possessions. They didn't even own the castle; it was on loan from the king in return for military and governmental service, and it could be taken away if the lord displeased the king in any way. However, the lord and lady did have their own bedroom, while the others slept on the floor of the great hall, alternately choking on smoke from the open fire and chilled by the drafts that came through the windows.

22. What is the main idea of this passage?

   Ⓐ Life in early England was dangerous and rough.
   Ⓑ Early English castles were unsafe places.
   Ⓒ Early English lords were unfair to their servants.
   Ⓓ Early English castles were not comfortable.

23. What was a main difference between the lord and the others in the castle?

   Ⓐ The lord was braver.
   Ⓑ He owned his home and they did not.
   Ⓒ The lord was richer.
   Ⓓ He was safer from danger of attack.

24. The author seems to feel that the lord's wife was —

   Ⓐ respected by everyone
   Ⓑ treated poorly
   Ⓒ destined to be wealthy
   Ⓓ educated well

25. Based on the information in this passage, what can you conclude about windows in early English castles?

   Ⓐ They did not shut tightly.
   Ⓑ They were covered with glass.
   Ⓒ There were many of them.
   Ⓓ They were very large.

GO ON

The alarm clock implanted in Klek 4's brain went off an hour too early. He wished he could turn over and go back to sleep, but the alarm was programmed to ring until he got up. He inched out of his sleepsack like a snail reluctantly leaving its shell.

Down in the kitchen, Klek entered "wheat toast/yogurt/orange" on the computer. The refrigerator doors opened, and two metal trays jerked forward, shooting a cup of strawberry yogurt and an orange into the air. "Watch it!" yelled Klek. He smelled burning toast. The whole system seemed to be malfunctioning today. "All right, all right," grumbled Klek. "I'll go into manual."

First he had to clean up the yogurt that spread like a gigantic blob on the floor. Then he had to bend over, pick up his orange, and peel it himself. Last he took two slices of wheat bread out of the anti-staleness unit and popped them into the toaster. He sat down at the table, sweating and breathing hard.

After breakfast, he was ready for school. He swallowed a brain improvement pill and turned on the learning screen. "Good morning," smiled a woman with red hair twisted into a tall spike. "This morning we will learn about Earth." The teacher had a loud, scratchy voice. Klek frowned and turned the Instructor Selection knob, erasing the woman from the screen and replacing her with a man with green, lizardlike skin. "Good morning," smiled the man. "This morning we will learn about Earth."

"Earth," Klek yawned. "How boring." He considered hooking the learning machine up to his head circuits, but decided against it. It would transfer the information instantly to his brain, but there was something creepy about knowing facts that he couldn't remember learning.

"Earth," stated the lizard-man, "was once a fertile planet inhabited by thousands of species, including human beings. Unfortunately, the humans polluted the planet so badly that they were forced to leave it and establish colonies here on Mars. Today, Earth shiguh shoomahc blaak urgh.." Klek smiled and hit *cancel*. Something had gone wrong with the sound again; there would be no more school for him until the machine was repaired, and that could take weeks. Everybody on Mars depended on machines, but only a handful of people knew how they worked.

With school out of the way, there was no reason not to play. Klek considered the alternatives. He could play chess with Klingsor, the Robotic ChessMaster. The only problem was that before you began a game you had to tell the system whether you wanted to win or lose, so no matter how exciting the game was, you knew how it would end.

He decided to play with his spaceship instead. Unfortunately, operating the toy required so much scientific knowledge that once Klek turned on Mission Control, the computer took over. He pushed the *on* button and watched the countdown. At "Zero!" the spaceship lifted off the floor and shot up to the ceiling, where it smashed to pieces. Klek sighed; it always happened that way, just when he was ready for a really exciting interplanetary voyage. He typed "Model Rocket Repair" into the telephone directory file, and the number came up on the screen.

GO ON

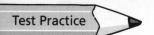

Reading Tryout Test 2 (continued)

26. What kind of story is this?

  (A) historical

  (B) animal

  (C) mystery

  (D) science fiction

27. Which of these events happened last?

  (A) Klek peeled an orange.

  (B) Klek put bread in the toaster.

  (C) Klek opened the refrigerator.

  (D) Klek swallowed a brain pill.

28. Why did Klek yell at the refrigerator?

  (A) It burned the toast.

  (B) The orange was warm.

  (C) It spilled the yogurt.

  (D) He didn't like the red-haired woman.

29. How did Klek feel when something went wrong with the learning machine?

  (A) sad

  (B) pleased

  (C) fascinated

  (D) enraged

30. Which generalization about the machines in Klek's house is supported by the story?

  (A) There are problems with all of them.

  (B) They are all implanted in his brain.

  (C) All are designed to play games.

  (D) All require complex training to operate.

31. Which word best describes Klek?

  (A) lazy

  (B) excitable

  (C) gloomy

  (D) brilliant

32. Why was Klek breathing hard and sweating when he sat down at the table?

  (A) It was very hot in the kitchen.

  (B) He was excited.

  (C) He was tired from making his breakfast.

  (D) He was nervous about doing his schoolwork.

33. "He inched out of his sleepsack like a snail reluctantly leaving its shell" means that —

  (A) Klek had turned into a snail during the night

  (B) Klek got out of bed very slowly

  (C) Klek's sleepsack looked like a snail's shell

  (D) Klek was only one inch long

34. What is the theme of this story?

  (A) It is foolish to depend too much on machines.

  (B) With patience, all problems can be solved.

  (C) Children need to spend more time playing and less time doing schoolwork.

  (D) Space travel is lonely and dangerous.

35. What will Klek most likely do next?

  (A) fix the spaceship

  (B) do his schoolwork

  (C) call the repair number

  (D) throw away the spaceship

Number Correct/Total = _____ /35

Language Arts

Top Ten Language Arts Tips

1 Read all DIRECTIONS through twice. Directions for language arts items often tell you to look for answer choices that have *mistakes* or *errors*. Other times, you are asked to look for the answer with *no mistakes*. It is important to know exactly what to look for.

2 Watch out for negative words in the directions, such as NOT or OPPOSITE. These words tell you exactly what answer to look for. Such words often appear in **bold** or *italic* type, or in ALL CAPITAL LETTERS.

3 When asked to answer questions about a reading passage, read the *questions* first. That way, you'll know what to look for as you read the passage. When you finish the passage, go on to answer the questions.

4 In language arts questions, look for key words, such as *who, what, when, where, why,* and *how,* that will help you answer each question. This is especially important when answering questions about maps, charts, and graphs or reference sources, such as dictionary entries, indexes, and tables of contents.

5 When answering questions about maps, charts, graphs, or reference sources, such as dictionary entries, always look back at the diagram or sample reference to answer the questions. Don't just rely on your memory.

6 Questions dealing with capitalization and punctuation can be tricky. The answer choices often look very much alike. Read *all* the answer choices, and choose your answer carefully.

7 For fill-in sentences, try each answer choice in the blank to see which one sounds right or makes the most sense.

8 For fill-in sentences, always read the entire sentence before you choose an answer. Use context clues, other words in the sentence that help define the unknown word, to find the correct answer.

9 When looking for word meanings, or definitions, use context clues to help you decide which definition of a word is best.

10 When asked to identify order of events, look for key words that signal time sequence, for example: *first, next, then, after, finally,* and *at last.*

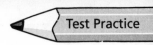
*This test will tell you how well you might score on a standardized language arts test **before** using this book.*

Language Arts Tryout Test 1

Time: **30** minutes

Directions: Follow the directions for each part of the test. Read each question carefully and fill in the circle beside the answer you choose. The answer to the sample question (**S**) has been filled in for you.

Questions 1–5. Choose the word or group of words that best completes the sentence.

S The man confessed his guilt, but the jury still _____ him not guilty.
- Ⓐ is finding
- Ⓒ founded
- Ⓑ have found
- ● found

1. The neighbors _____ a big picnic every year on Labor Day.
- Ⓐ hold
- Ⓒ has held
- Ⓑ holds
- Ⓓ is holding

2. _____ are about the same size.
- Ⓐ Me and her
- Ⓒ I and her
- Ⓑ He and me
- Ⓓ She and I

3. "Each boy has to get _____ parents' permission," said Nick.
- Ⓐ our
- Ⓒ my
- Ⓑ their
- Ⓓ his

4. Lou is the _____ of three sons.
- Ⓐ youngest
- Ⓒ most young
- Ⓑ younger
- Ⓓ most youngest

5. The pilot _____ see the runway.
- Ⓐ hardly
- Ⓒ couldn't hardly
- Ⓑ could hardly
- Ⓓ could hardly not

Questions 6–8. Read the four groups of words. Choose the one that is a complete sentence written correctly.

6. Ⓐ Last week when my friend Cara came to visit.
   Ⓑ She left her jacket on a chair in the front hall.
   Ⓒ A little later the jacket walked into the room we were so surprised!
   Ⓓ We spotted my dog's tail sticking out, we knew what had happened.

7. Ⓐ Jackie worked hard on his report, it was finally finished.
   Ⓑ Nearly a hundred pages of text, diagrams, and tables.
   Ⓒ A sudden gust of wind that snatched the report out of Jackie's hands.
   Ⓓ Fortunately, Jackie had remembered to number the pages.

8. Ⓐ A strong, cold wind from the northeast swept across the plains.
   Ⓑ The two boys huddled together, they wished they were home at their camp.
   Ⓒ Their father, Chief Strong Bow, worrying as he looked out across the empty land.
   Ⓓ There is a storm coming I have to go out and find those boys.

GO ON

Language Arts Tryout Test 1 (continued)

Questions 9–10. Read the underlined sentences. Choose the answer that best combines them into one clear sentence without changing their meaning.

9. The apartment didn't have a stove.
    The apartment didn't have a refrigerator, either.

    Ⓐ The apartment didn't have neither a stove nor a refrigerator.

    Ⓑ The apartment didn't have a stove and a refrigerator.

    Ⓒ The apartment didn't have a stove or a refrigerator.

    Ⓓ The apartment didn't have a stove, it didn't have a refrigerator, either.

10. I stared at the sow.
    The sow was much larger than I had imagined.

    Ⓐ I stared at the sow, which was much larger than I had imagined.

    Ⓑ Much larger than I had imagined, I stared at the sow.

    Ⓒ I stared at the sow, the sow being much larger than I had imagined.

    Ⓓ The sow was much larger than I had imagined, so I stared at her.

Questions 11–12. Read each paragraph and answer the question.

11.   Many people make the mistake of judging animal behavior by human standards, attaching human motives and feelings to purely instinctive acts. For example, a salmon is driven by instinct to return to the place where it was hatched in order to mate; its upstream journey is often described as "determined" or "courageous." It would be more accurate to compare the fish to a log carried along by a strong current. _____

    Which sentence best fills the blank in the paragraph?

    Ⓐ One need only observe a newborn baby to realize that humans also are born with strong instinctive behaviors.

    Ⓑ The analogies between humans and animals can help non-scientists understand the complex world of animal behavior.

    Ⓒ In contrast, the tricks performed at marine zoos by dolphins and other sea mammals are examples of learned behavior.

    Ⓓ By describing other species in human terms, we undervalue the qualities and characteristics that make each species unique.

12. [1]"Excuse me, Mr. Sims," said the butler, "but you were due at the Smiths' a half hour ago."

    [2]"Yes, young people nowadays think nothing of showing up ten minutes late for an appointment," agreed Rawlins.

    [3]"Punctuality is a lost virtue," commented Archibald Sims to his friend Rawlins.

    [4]The two friends went on to discuss the chronic lateness of their friends and associates, until the butler interrupted.

    Which arrangement of the sentences would make the best paragraph?

    Ⓐ 3 – 2 – 4 – 1   Ⓑ 4 – 1 – 3 – 2   Ⓒ 2 – 3 – 4 – 1   Ⓓ 4 – 2 – 3 – 1

GO ON

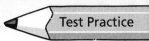

Questions 13–16. Read the phrases. In one of the phrases, the underlined word is misspelled for the way it is used. Choose the phrase in which the underlined word is NOT spelled correctly.

13. Ⓐ a <u>bass</u> guitar
    Ⓑ to <u>alter</u> a suit
    Ⓒ New Year's <u>Eave</u>
    Ⓓ <u>bowled</u> a perfect game

14. Ⓐ ice cream <u>sundae</u>
    Ⓑ a <u>metal</u> detector
    Ⓒ <u>principal</u> of the school
    Ⓓ bad table <u>manors</u>

15. Ⓐ a bank <u>loan</u>
    Ⓑ the <u>bow</u> of the tree
    Ⓒ <u>pare</u> an apple
    Ⓓ an <u>aisle</u> seat

16. Ⓐ a ripped <u>seam</u>
    Ⓑ <u>grate</u> some cheese
    Ⓒ a floor that <u>creeks</u>
    Ⓓ <u>told</u> a lie

Questions 17–22. Read each group of sentences. Choose the sentence that uses correct punctuation and capitalization.

17. Ⓐ On Friday nights, my friends and I like to watch old movies on television.
    Ⓑ Our favorites are monster movies the ones that are so bad that they're funny.
    Ⓒ We make popcorn stay up late and get very silly.
    Ⓓ Joel, who wants to be an actor imitates the different characters.

18. Ⓐ Benjamin Franklin played many roles in colonial America: printer, publisher, postmaster, inventor, diplomat, and statesman.
    Ⓑ He published *The pennsylvania gazette* for almost 40 years.
    Ⓒ His most successful publication was Poor Richard's Almanac.
    Ⓓ The almanac included original proverbs such as "a penny saved is a penny earned."

19. Ⓐ My family is moving to Boise Idaho next summer.
    Ⓑ Dad's company is moving its headquarters there.
    Ⓒ The good news is that dad will be getting a promotion.
    Ⓓ it will be hard to say goodbye to my friends.

20. Ⓐ Lucy was puzzled to receive a letter with an italian postmark.
    Ⓑ The letter, which was from her friend Joe, began, "Dear Lucia."
    Ⓒ Lucy wondered what Joe was doing in Italy?
    Ⓓ It turned out that he had a new job in Rome; and had just arrived.

21. Ⓐ The School Librarian was retiring after forty years on the job!
    Ⓑ The students at BJ Wilder Elementary School gave her a big party.
    Ⓒ Many of Mrs Lee's former students attended the party.
    Ⓓ The Garden Club planted flowers in her honor in Kingsville Park.

22. Ⓐ "Hello, Mark," said a strange voice on the telephone.
    Ⓑ "This is your Uncle Fred calling from Oregon"
    Ⓒ "Ill be in town next week and would like to stop by for a visit."
    Ⓓ Mark said politely, "I'm sorry sir, but you must have the wrong number. I don't have an Uncle Fred."

GO ON

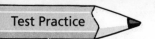

Language Arts Tryout Test 1 (continued)

Questions 23–25. Use the sample outline to answer each question.

> Thailand
> I.   Geography
>   A. Land and Water
>   B. Climate
>   C. Natural Resources
>   D. Manufacturing
> II. History
> III. _____
> IV. Economy
>   A. Agriculture
>   B. Industries
> V.   Culture
>   A. Education
>   B. _____
>   C. The Arts
>   D. Folk Customs

23. Which heading would best fit in the blank at III?
    Ⓐ Government
    Ⓑ Environment
    Ⓒ The King
    Ⓓ Money

24. Which subheading would best fit in the blank beside V–B?
    Ⓐ Forestry
    Ⓑ King's Role in Government
    Ⓒ Religion
    Ⓓ Effects of World War II

25. Which subheading does NOT belong under heading I?
    Ⓐ A. Land and Water
    Ⓑ B. Climate
    Ⓒ C. Natural Resources
    Ⓓ D. Manufacturing

Questions 26–29. Use the sample dictionary entries to answer each question.

> **chip·munk** (chĭp′ mŭngk) *n.* a small North American squirrel with striped markings on the head and back, living mainly on the ground. [Algonquian]
>
> **chi·rop·ter** (kĭ rŏp′ tər) *n.* a member of the bat family. [Gr *cheir*, hand + *pteron*, wing]
>
> **chirr** (chŭr) *n.* a sharp, trilling sound, like that made by a grasshopper. *v.* to make such a sound. [Imitative]
>
> **chis·el** (chĭz′ əl) *n.* a hand tool with a sharp blade for cutting or shaping wood, stone, etc. *v.* To cut or shape, using a chisel [OFr *cisel* < L *caesus*, to cut]

26. A *chirr* is a —
    Ⓐ bat
    Ⓑ sound
    Ⓒ grasshopper
    Ⓓ wing

27. What part of speech is the word *chiropter*?
    Ⓐ adjective
    Ⓑ adverb
    Ⓒ noun
    Ⓓ verb

28. The word *chipmunk* comes from what language?
    Ⓐ Greek
    Ⓑ Old French
    Ⓒ Latin
    Ⓓ Algonquian

29. These words would appear on the same dictionary page as which set of guide words?
    Ⓐ chintz – chit
    Ⓑ chill – Chinese
    Ⓒ chivalry – choir
    Ⓓ chrism – chubby

GO ON

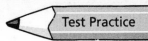

Questions 30–32. Use the graph to answer each question.

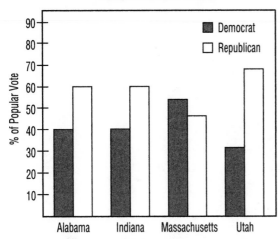

1988 PRESIDENTIAL ELECTION RESULTS IN SELECTED STATES

30. About what percent of the vote did the Republican candidate win in Massachusetts?

   Ⓐ 55   Ⓒ 45
   Ⓑ 50   Ⓓ 30

31. In which state did the Democratic candidate win the largest percentage of the vote?

   Ⓐ Alabama   Ⓒ Massachusetts
   Ⓑ Indiana   Ⓓ Utah

32. Which question could be answered using the information in this graph?

   Ⓐ In which of these states was the Democratic candidate most successful?
   Ⓑ Which candidate was elected President?
   Ⓒ How many Alabamans voted for the Republican candidate?
   Ⓓ Why did Massachusetts tend to vote for the Democrat?

Questions 33–36. Choose the best answer to each question.

33. If you wanted to learn about yesterday's election results, you would look in —

   Ⓐ an almanac
   Ⓑ a telephone directory
   Ⓒ an encyclopedia
   Ⓓ a newspaper

34. If you want to find the meaning of an unfamiliar word used in a textbook, you should look in the —

   Ⓐ glossary
   Ⓑ thesaurus
   Ⓒ index
   Ⓓ bibliography

35. To find a book with information on Abraham Lincoln's Congressional career, you should look in the card catalog under —

   Ⓐ Abraham
   Ⓑ Lincoln
   Ⓒ Congress
   Ⓓ President

36. If you want to find out which states share their borders with Mexico, you should look in —

   Ⓐ an almanac
   Ⓑ an encyclopedia
   Ⓒ a dictionary
   Ⓓ an atlas

Number Correct/Total = _____ /36

59

Parts of Speech

Identifying and using correct word forms in sentences

Directions: Read each sentence. Choose the word or group of words that belongs in the blank.

A Last Friday the Jolsons _____ for a week's vacation.

    Ⓐ leaves

    Ⓑ left

    Ⓒ leaved

    Ⓓ has left

B Jackie is the _____ girl on the basketball team.

    Ⓐ taller

    Ⓑ more tall

    Ⓒ tallest

    Ⓓ most tall

Example A tests the use of **verbs**, or "action words." The phrase "Last Friday" gives you a clue. It tells you that you need a past tense form of the verb. Answer Ⓒ, *leaved*, is an incorrect way to write the past tense. The correct answer is Ⓑ, *left*.

Example B is a question about **adjectives**, or "describing words." Since the sentence compares more than two things (the height of all the girls on the team), the correct form should end in *est*. Choice Ⓒ, *tallest*, is correct. If the sentence compared only two things, then the correct answer would end in *er*, *taller*.

Now let's look at another kind of question.

Directions: Read each group of sentences. Choose the sentence that is written correctly.

C   Ⓐ Mackenzie couldn't get no sleep last night.

    Ⓑ She didn't hardly shut her eyes all night.

    Ⓒ Counting sheep wasn't no help.

    Ⓓ Nothing she tried did her any good.

In this kind of question, you are looking for the correct sentence. Sentence Ⓓ is written correctly. The other three sentences have mistakes in using negative words.

taller

tall

Language Rules

▶ Use the correct form of the verb to show when an action takes place.

It **happened** in the past. It **happens** in the present.

It **will happen** in the future.

▶ Make sure the verb agrees with the subject.

She likes ice cream. **They like** ice cream.

▶ Use the comparative form of adjectives and adverbs when comparing two things.

He is **braver** than I. He is **more courageous**.

▶ Use the superlative form when comparing more than two things.

He is the **bravest** boy I know. He is the **most courageous** of all.

▶ For most one-syllable words, use the *er* or *est* ending (braver, bravest). For most words of more than one syllable, use the word *more* or *most* (more courageous, most courageous).

▶ Use a subject pronoun for the subject of a sentence: *I, we, you, they, he, she.*

She and **I** went to the carnival.

▶ Use an object pronoun as the object in a sentence: *me, us, you, them, him,* and *her.*

Susanne gave the book to **me**.

▶ Make sure the pronoun agrees with the word it refers to.

One of the boys lost **his** hat. **Both** boys lost **their** hats.

▶ Use only one negative in a sentence.

Counting sheep was **no** help.

tallest

Test-Taking Tips

1 Try out each answer by reading the sentence to yourself. If the sentence sounds odd, it is probably wrong.

2 Watch out for irregular forms (such as *left*, not *leaved*) and spelling changes (*prettier*, not *prettyer*).

3 Be alert for the most common kinds of mistakes (such as "Us kids like ice cream for dessert" instead of "We kids like ice cream for dessert").

Go for it

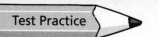

Test Practice 1: Parts of Speech

Time: **15** minutes

Questions 1–10. Read each sentence. Choose the word or group of words that best completes the sentence.

1. Chelsey and her friends _____ to the Steeltop concert last night.

   Ⓐ gone
   Ⓑ have gone
   Ⓒ went
   Ⓓ have went

2. One of Jason's uncles _____ professional football.

   Ⓐ are playing
   Ⓑ play
   Ⓒ have played
   Ⓓ plays

3. You must speak _____ if you want people to understand you.

   Ⓐ clear
   Ⓑ clearly
   Ⓒ clearlier
   Ⓓ clearest

4. The Do-Stop-In Diner served the _____ rhubarb pie that Mr. Dooley had ever eaten.

   Ⓐ tasty
   Ⓑ tastier
   Ⓒ tastiest
   Ⓓ more tasty

5. Neither the police _____ the FBI had ever heard of the Blue Brigade before.

   Ⓐ nor
   Ⓑ and
   Ⓒ or
   Ⓓ but

6. I promised that _____ would help with the refreshments.

   Ⓐ she and I
   Ⓑ her and I
   Ⓒ I and she
   Ⓓ her and me

7. "Each girl has to buy _____ own uniform," Vicki told her mom.

   Ⓐ our
   Ⓑ her
   Ⓒ their
   Ⓓ my

8. In the four months he had lived in the house, Mr. Baylor _____ looked in the hall closet.

   Ⓐ hadn't not
   Ⓑ hadn't not ever
   Ⓒ hadn't never
   Ⓓ had never

9. Collin _____ building his new cabinet, but he has not yet painted it.

   Ⓐ has finished
   Ⓑ will finish
   Ⓒ is finishing
   Ⓓ had finished

10. Jana gave _____ a ride to the station, and we took the 4:30 train.

    Ⓐ he and I
    Ⓑ him and I
    Ⓒ he and me
    Ⓓ him and me

GO ON

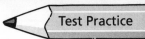

Questions 11–16. Read each group of sentences. Choose the sentence that is written correctly.

11. Ⓐ Yesterday I gone to the shopping mall for a haircut.
    Ⓑ When I got there, I notice something strange.
    Ⓒ I change my mind as soon as I seen their spiked purple hair.
    Ⓓ Tomorrow I will try the new barber shop on Main Street instead.

12. Ⓐ Each of the passengers goes through a security check at the gate.
    Ⓑ Only people with boarding passes is allowed to go on the airplane.
    Ⓒ Anyone who is meeting passengers have to go to the waiting area.
    Ⓓ Most of the waiting area windows looks out on the runway.

13. Ⓐ I arrived lately for the gymnastics meet on Saturday.
    Ⓑ I went into the gym and took my seat quick.
    Ⓒ All of the gymnasts in the meet performed very good.
    Ⓓ The winner did some very unusual stunts.

14. Ⓐ The janitor just had finished mopping the entire building.
    Ⓑ The new manager ordered him to wash the floor again sternly.
    Ⓒ The janitor unhappily got out his bucket, mop, and sponges.
    Ⓓ Then he decided the manager would get only worse, so he quit.

15. Ⓐ The mastodon and the mammoth were prehistoric animals related to the elephant.
    Ⓑ The mastodon had tusks like an elephant's, and its teeth were different.
    Ⓒ Fossils from both the mastodon and also the mammoth have been found in North America.
    Ⓓ Unfortunately, the local museum does not have either mastodon nor mammoth fossils on display.

16. Ⓐ Teresa and me have been friends for a long time.
    Ⓑ We met when she and her family moved into the house next door.
    Ⓒ Her sister used to babysit for my brother and I.
    Ⓓ Us kids played together every day from sunrise to sunset.

Number Correct/Total = _____ /16

63

Sentences

Recognizing subjects, predicates,
and complete sentences

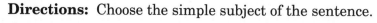

Directions: Choose the simple subject of the sentence.

A That little <u>boy</u> <u>likes</u> <u>vanilla</u> better than any other <u>flavor</u>.
        Ⓐ   Ⓑ   Ⓒ   Ⓓ

Example A asks you to find the underlined part of the sentence that is the simple subject. The **simple subject** is the person or thing that performs the action of the sentence. In this sentence, *likes* is the action. The simple subject is *boy*. He is the person who likes vanilla. Choice Ⓐ is the correct answer. Choice Ⓑ, *likes*, is the predicate. Choice Ⓒ, *vanilla*, is the object of *likes*. Choice Ⓓ, *flavor*, is part of the complete predicate.

Some questions ask for the complete subject. The words that come before the action word are the **complete subject**. In this sentence, the complete subject is *That little boy*. The action word and the words that come after it form the **complete predicate**.

Now look at this example.

Directions: Choose the simple predicate of the sentence.

B <u>Coach Weiss</u> <u>blew</u> his <u>whistle</u> when the ball <u>went</u> out of bounds.
      Ⓐ   Ⓑ   Ⓒ   Ⓓ

Example B asks for the simple predicate. The **simple predicate** is the verb that tells about the action of the sentence. In this sentence the simple predicate is *blew*, choice Ⓑ. The action is performed by *Coach Weiss*, the subject of the sentence. Choice Ⓒ, *whistle*, is the object of *blew*. Choice Ⓓ, *went*, is also a verb, but it is not the predicate. In this sentence, it is part of the adverb phrase "when the ball went out of bounds," which tells when Coach Weiss blew the whistle. The complete predicate would be "blew his whistle when the ball went out of bounds."

Here is another example.

Directions: Read the four groups of words. Choose the one that is a complete sentence written correctly.

C Ⓐ *Dragonfire* is a terrible movie don't waste your time seeing it.

    Ⓑ The script was foolish, the actors made it even worse.

    Ⓒ When you think of all the money that went into making *Dragonfire*.

    Ⓓ This movie proves that millions of dollars cannot buy good acting.

A **sentence** has a subject and a verb, and it expresses a complete thought. Choice Ⓓ is the correct answer. It has a subject (*movie*) and a verb (*proves*), and it expresses a complete thought.

Choices Ⓐ and Ⓑ are run-on sentences. A **run-on** sentence actually contains two or more sentences run together without correct punctuation. Choice Ⓒ is a sentence **fragment**. It is a part of a sentence that does not express a complete thought.

Hints

Look at these examples of a run-on sentence and a sentence fragment. Each one has been rewritten correctly.

Run-on sentence:
Thank you for the water I was really thirsty.

Correct:
Thank you for the water. I was really thirsty.
Thank you for the water; I was really thirsty.

Sentence fragment:
One day when I had nothing to do.

Correct:
One day when I had nothing to do, I went for a walk.

SENTENCE

Test-Taking Tips

1 When looking for the subject, look for the person or thing that performs the action of the sentence. *Who* is acting?

2 When looking for the predicate, look for the action. *What* is the subject doing?

3 Some sentences are confusing because of the way they are written, as in "There is the one that I told you about." If you run into one of these, rearrange the sentence in your mind so you can see the subject or the predicate. (The *one* that I told you about is there.)

4 When looking for a complete sentence, watch out for a group of words that does not express a complete thought, or is missing the subject or predicated. This is a sentence fragment: *Going by the school at 3:00* (there is no subject).

5 Watch out for two or more sentences run together. This is a run-on sentence: *It is autumn the leaves are turning color and falling.* (two subjects, two predicates; no punctuation separating them).

6 Make sure that the answer you choose has a subject and a verb and expresses one complete thought.

Go for it

Test Practice 2: Sentences   Time: 16 minutes

Questions 1–6. Choose the simple subject of each sentence.

1. Many people think of zoos simply as fun places to visit.
   Ⓐ   Ⓑ   Ⓒ   Ⓓ

2. A good zoo also serves an important educational function.
         Ⓐ   Ⓑ   Ⓒ   Ⓓ

3. By helping to educate humans about other species, the animals
                          Ⓐ   Ⓑ   Ⓒ

   in zoos play a crucial role in efforts to preserve those species.
      Ⓓ

4. The star of Taft High School's basketball team this year is an
       Ⓐ   Ⓑ   Ⓒ

   energetic six-foot sophomore named Barry McAllister.
                      Ⓓ

5. In spite of a slow start, McAllister was the state's highest scorer.
                      Ⓐ   Ⓑ   Ⓒ   Ⓓ

6. In the last game of the season, he made an amazing half-court
              Ⓐ   Ⓑ   Ⓒ

   shot just as the buzzer sounded.
   Ⓓ

Questions 7–12. Choose the simple predicate of each sentence.

7. Winding lazily through scenic green hills, the Crystal River
    Ⓐ   Ⓑ

   provides the ideal setting for a slow-paced vacation.
      Ⓒ   Ⓓ

8. Canoes are the preferred form of transportation on Crystal River.
    Ⓐ   Ⓑ   Ⓒ   Ⓓ

9. The river's fish have grown fat on the bait of dozing fishermen.
              Ⓐ   Ⓑ   Ⓒ   Ⓓ

10. The approaching sound of a marching band alerted the crowd.
          Ⓐ   Ⓑ   Ⓒ   Ⓓ

11. Blaring trumpets and booming bass drums mixed with the gentler
     Ⓐ   Ⓑ   Ⓒ

    tones of flutes and piccolos.
    Ⓓ

12. Acrobatic clowns tumbled down the street between the colorful floats.
                      Ⓐ   Ⓑ   Ⓒ   Ⓓ

GO ON

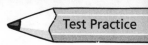

Questions 13–20. For each question, read the four groups of words. Choose the one that is a complete sentence written correctly.

13. Ⓐ My mother grew up in New York, my father grew up there, too.
    Ⓑ Whenever I visit my grandmother and grandfather in Brooklyn.
    Ⓒ Every inch of their walls covered with family photographs.
    Ⓓ Grandma and Grandpa love to tell stories about the family.

14. Ⓐ A good idea to have your teeth checked by a dentist twice a year.
    Ⓑ Today's dentists work to prevent dental problems before they occur.
    Ⓒ Brushing your teeth is not enough it is important to floss as well.
    Ⓓ Considering the importance of healthy teeth for overall well-being.

15. Ⓐ Fifty million years ago, the land bridge connecting Australia to Asia was cut off.
    Ⓑ As a result, many animals that live in Australia and nowhere else.
    Ⓒ One odd animal is the platypus it is a web-footed mammal that lays eggs.
    Ⓓ The males have an unusual defense mechanism, they scratch their enemies with poison-filled claws.

16. Ⓐ Neang had some spare time, he also had some spare change.
    Ⓑ The video arcade at the mall, which had "Star-Blasters" and "Tyor."
    Ⓒ Until then, his best "Star-Blasters" score of 159,000 points.
    Ⓓ When he scored 240,000, even Neang himself was surprised.

17. Ⓐ Liechtenstein, one of the smallest countries in the world since it became independent in 1806.
    Ⓑ Smaller in area than Washington, D.C., and its population is only about 30,000.
    Ⓒ Two hydroelectric plants supply power for the entire country, they also sell power to neighboring countries.
    Ⓓ Located between Austria and Switzerland, Liechtenstein shares many of the characteristics of both its neighbors.

18. Ⓐ Vinegar makes great salad dressing it has many other uses as well.
    Ⓑ A teaspoonful in your dog's water to help repel fleas and ticks.
    Ⓒ White vinegar is a soothing remedy for insect bites and sunburn.
    Ⓓ For sparkling windows, a mixture of white vinegar and water.

19. Ⓐ Mardi and Janette going into business together.
    Ⓑ They repair broken toys they also mend torn clothing.
    Ⓒ According to their sign, they can fix anything.
    Ⓓ How they learned to repair so many different kinds of items.

20. Ⓐ Thousands of children have read and enjoyed *The Jungle Book.*
    Ⓑ The author, Rudyard Kipling, who grew up in India himself.
    Ⓒ Many of his books about India and other parts of the British Empire.
    Ⓓ Kipling defended colonialism, he became unpopular because of this.

Number Correct/Total = _____ /20

Combining Sentences

Revising sentences by combining them

Directions: Read the underlined sentences. Choose the answer that best combines them into one clear sentence without changing their meaning.

<u>Karen liked Bach.</u>
<u>Karen liked Mozart even better.</u>

Ⓐ Karen liked Bach, and Karen liked Mozart even better.

Ⓑ Karen liked Bach, she liked Mozart even better.

Ⓒ Karen liked Bach, but she liked Mozart even better.

Ⓓ Karen liked both Bach and Mozart.

In questions like this one, you have to choose the best way to combine the sentences. The new sentence should have the same meaning as the original sentences, and it should be well constructed.

In the example, the correct answer is Ⓒ. It has the same meaning as the original sentences, and it is well written. Answer choice Ⓐ does combine the sentences, but the result is not well constructed because it unnecessarily repeats *Karen liked*. Choice Ⓑ is a run-on sentence. Choice Ⓓ changes the meaning of the original sentences.

Language Rules

These kinds of test questions usually combine sentences by combining subjects, predicates, objects, or modifiers. Look at these examples.

Marcus bought a new skateboard. Charlene bought a new skateboard.
Combined subjects: Marcus and Charlene bought new skateboards.

Marcus painted his skateboard black. He added decals to the skateboard.
Combined predicates: Marcus painted his skateboard black and added decals.

Carlita knitted a sweater for me. She made me a new hat, too.
Combined objects: Carlita knitted a new hat and sweater for me.

Tony found his new shoes. His new shoes were under the bed.
Combined modifiers: Tony found his new shoes under the bed.

Test-Taking Tips

1 Make sure the sentence you choose is well constructed and does not change the meaning of the original sentences.

2 Look at the conjunctions closely (*and*, *but*, *or*, etc.). The wrong conjunction changes the meaning of the sentence.

(Example: *We wanted to go skating and sledding, but it looked like a blizzard was coming.* vs. *We wanted to go skating or sledding, and it looked like a blizzard was coming.*)

Go for it

Test Practice 3: Combining Sentences

Time: **10** minutes

Directions: Read the underlined sentences. Choose the answer that best combines them into one clear sentence without changing their meaning.

1. Jensen plays on the soccer team.
   Ruiz plays on the soccer team.

   Ⓐ Jensen plays on the soccer team, and Ruiz plays on the
       soccer team.
   Ⓑ Jensen and Ruiz both play on the soccer team.
   Ⓒ Jensen and Ruiz both play on soccer teams.
   Ⓓ Jensen plays on the soccer team, Ruiz plays on the soccer
       team, too.

2. I lent Cary a book last month.
   Cary returned the book.

   Ⓐ Cary returned the book that I lent him last month.
   Ⓑ Cary returned the book, I lent it to him last month.
   Ⓒ Cary returned the book last month that I lent him.
   Ⓓ I lent Cary the book that he returned last month.

3. We were late for the movie.
   The movie started at 7:15.

   Ⓐ At 7:15, we were late for the movie.
   Ⓑ We were late for the movie, and it started at 7:15.
   Ⓒ The movie that started at 7:15 is the one we were late for.
   Ⓓ We were late for the movie, which started at 7:15.

4. I saw an unusual bird.
   The bird was on the bird feeder.

   Ⓐ I saw an unusual bird on the bird feeder.
   Ⓑ The unusual bird that I saw was the one on the bird feeder.
   Ⓒ I saw an unusual bird, it was on the bird feeder.
   Ⓓ On the bird feeder was an unusual bird.

5. Galveston is in Texas.
   It was nearly destroyed by a hurricane in 1900.

   Ⓐ Galveston, Texas, was nearly destroyed; a hurricane hit it
       in 1900.
   Ⓑ In Texas, Galveston was nearly destroyed by a hurricane
       in 1900.
   Ⓒ Galveston, Texas, was nearly destroyed by a hurricane in 1900.
   Ⓓ In 1900 a hurricane nearly destroyed Galveston, which is
       in Texas.

GO ON

6. Marjy could not watch TV.
   She had not finished her homework.

   Ⓐ Marjy finished her homework; then she could watch TV.
   Ⓑ Marjy could not watch TV because she had not finished her homework.
   Ⓒ After Marjy finished her homework, she could watch TV.
   Ⓓ Marjy could not watch TV, and she had not finished her homework.

7. Lewis Carroll loved children.
   He had no children of his own.

   Ⓐ Having no children of his own, Lewis Carroll loved children.
   Ⓑ Lewis Carroll loved children but had none of his own.
   Ⓒ Although Lewis Carroll had no children of his own, he loved them.
   Ⓓ Lewis Carroll loved children, and he had none of his own.

8. The job sounded interesting.
   Dan decided to apply for the job.

   Ⓐ The job sounded interesting, so Dan decided to apply for it.
   Ⓑ The job, which sounded interesting, Dan decided to apply for.
   Ⓒ The job sounded interesting, but Dan decided to apply for it.
   Ⓓ Dan decided to apply for an interesting-sounding job.

9. The Incas constructed some remarkable buildings.
   The buildings are high in the Andes Mountains.

   Ⓐ The Incas, who lived high in the Andes Mountains, constructed some remarkable buildings.
   Ⓑ The remarkable buildings constructed by the Incas are high in the Andes Mountains.
   Ⓒ The Incas constructed some remarkable buildings high in the Andes Mountains.
   Ⓓ High in the Andes Mountains are some buildings remarkably constructed by the Incas.

10. Robert E. Lee was a skilled military leader.
    Lee was unable to win victory for the Confederacy.

    Ⓐ Robert E. Lee was a skilled military leader, Lee was unable to win victory for the Confederacy.
    Ⓑ Robert E. Lee was a skilled military leader unable to win victory for the Confederacy.
    Ⓒ Robert E. Lee was a skilled military leader and was unable to win victory for the Confederacy.
    Ⓓ Robert E. Lee was a skilled military leader, but he was unable to win victory for the Confederacy.

Number Correct/Total = _____ /10

Writing Paragraphs

Completing paragraphs and arranging sentences in order

Directions: Read the paragraph below. Then answer the question.

A   Nellie Bly was an adventuresome reporter. She once pretended to be insane so that she could learn about the treatment of patients in a New York mental hospital. _____ In other cases, the stories she wrote helped to bring about badly needed reforms.

Which sentence best fits the blank in the paragraph?

  Ⓐ   She began writing articles for *The Pittsburgh Dispatch* when she was only 18 years old.

  Ⓑ   In 1890 she set a record by completing a trip around the world in a little over 72 days.

  Ⓒ   "Nellie Bly" was just a pen name; her real name was Elizabeth Cochrane Seaman.

  Ⓓ   She also got herself arrested so that she could report on the police's treatment of women prisoners.

This question asks you to choose the sentence that best fits into the paragraph. The first sentence in the paragraph says that Nellie Bly was *an adventuresome reporter*. The second sentence gives an example of one of her adventures. Then the last sentence refers to *both cases*. These clues tell you that the missing sentence should be about another adventure. Choice Ⓓ is the correct answer.

Most paragraphs have a topic sentence which introduces the main idea, and several detail sentences to support or illustrate the main idea. This example question asks you to find the missing detail sentence. Other common types of questions ask you to choose the best topic sentence or identify the sentence that does NOT belong in a paragraph.

Now let's look at a different kind of example.

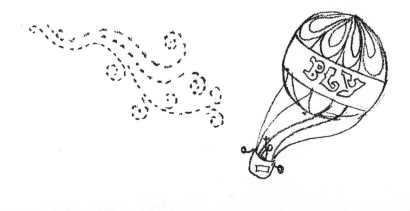

Nellie continued her amazing journey

Directions: Read the paragraph and answer the question that follows.

B ¹Then she silently turned the knob and slowly pushed open the front door.

²Carla slipped off her shoes on the darkened front porch.

³With a sigh of relief, she finally sneaked into her own room, where she found her mother and father waiting for her.

⁴Holding her breath, she tiptoed up the stairs and past her parents' room.

Which arrangement of the sentences would make the best paragraph?

Ⓐ 1 – 2 – 3 – 4   Ⓒ 2 – 4 – 1 – 3
Ⓑ 2 – 1 – 4 – 3   Ⓓ 1 – 4 – 2 – 3

In this type of question, you have to decide how the sentences are related to each other. In Example B, you have to figure out a sequence of events that makes logical sense. Picture Carla's movement through the house as she tries to sneak in late: porch, front door, parents' room, her room. Choice Ⓑ is the correct answer.

In most of these questions, the sentences will either describe a sequence of events or a set of procedures. The sequence of events follows a chronological, or time, order. The set of procedures might be a set of directions in which the steps must be taken in a certain logical order.

Test-Taking Tips

1 Figure out the main idea of the paragraph first. Then look for the detail sentence that fits the rest of the paragraph.

2 In questions that ask for the best topic sentence, figure out the topic or main idea of the paragraph by looking for a common thread among the sentences.

3 Look for clue words and phrases, such as *then, as a result, in this case,* and *on the other hand.*

4 Figure out the correct order first, and write down the numbers of the sentences in a list. Then match your list to an answer.

5 If the sentences tell a story, find the sequence of events.

6 If the sentences describe a procedure, such as a set of directions, find the logical order of steps.

7 Look for clue words and phrases, such as *first, next, then, after that, before, until, last, finally* (see sentences 1 and 3 in Example B).

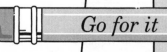

Go for it

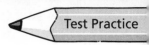

Test Practice 4 : Writing Paragraphs   Time: 8 minutes

Directions: Read each paragraph and answer the question that follows.

1.   Quebec, the largest of Canada's ten provinces, differs from the others in one important way. Over 80 percent of its residents are of French, rather than British, descent, and many speak French as their main or only language. _____ As a result, many Quebec citizens favor the idea of seceding from Canada and forming a separate country.

Which sentence best fits the blank in the paragraph?

Ⓐ Relations between Quebec and the English-speaking provinces were very tense during the two world wars.

Ⓑ Millions of tourists visit Quebec each year.

Ⓒ France turned control of Canada over to Great Britain in 1763.

Ⓓ This cultural difference between Quebec and the rest of Canada has created political problems over the years.

2.   A critical element of applying for a job is the letter you send with your resume or application. A good cover letter persuades the recipient to look at the rest of your application. State clearly but briefly why you are interested in the job and what your qualifications are. _____

Which sentence best fits the blank in the paragraph?

Ⓐ Dress neatly and arrive on time for your interview.

Ⓑ Your resume should list your major school and community activities.

Ⓒ Make sure your letter is correctly punctuated and neatly typed.

Ⓓ Look the interviewer in the eye and speak in a clear, firm voice.

3.   [1]Although knives and spoons have been in use since the days of the cave dwellers, forks are a relatively recent invention. [2]The earliest knives were made out of stone. [3]When they first appeared in the eleventh century, forks were considered scandalous and were denounced by the Church. [4]As late as the seventeenth century, the use of a fork was considered cause for ridicule. [5]It was not until the late eighteenth century that forks came into common use.

Which sentence does NOT belong in the paragraph?

Ⓐ 2   Ⓑ 3   Ⓒ 4   Ⓓ 5

4.   [1]On certain days it seemed as though winter had frozen in place. [2]A swirling mist of snow was the only hint of movement on the hard, bare landscape. [3]The sun struggled to clear the hills, lingered gloomily, and sank below the horizon again. [4]Skiers in bright clothing called gaily to each other as they raced toward the cheerfully lit cabin.

Which sentence does NOT belong in the paragraph?

Ⓐ 1   Ⓑ 2   Ⓒ 3   Ⓓ 4

 GO ON

5. _____ There are many natural controls. One of the best is companion planting, in which plants that repel certain insects are sown near plants most likely to be attacked by those same insects. For example, Mexican bean beetles hate potatoes. Plant potatoes near your beans and you have instant protection for your beans!

Which is the best topic sentence for this paragraph?

Ⓐ Ladybugs and praying mantises help the gardener by eating other insects.

Ⓑ It is not necessary to use chemicals to control garden pests.

Ⓒ A protective spray for the garden can be made from ground-up marigolds mixed with water.

Ⓓ Most common garden chemicals are safe if used properly.

6. _____ In 1587 a group of English colonists settled on the island. Their leader, John White, sailed back to England for supplies but was delayed there for over two years. When he finally returned in 1590, the colonists had vanished. The word CROATOAN carved into a tree was the only clue to their disappearance.

Which is the best topic sentence for this paragraph?

Ⓐ The first attempt to settle Roanoke Island took place in 1585.

Ⓑ No one knows what became of the Lost Colony of Roanoke Island.

Ⓒ English colonists in the New World faced many hardships.

Ⓓ Roanoke Island in North Carolina has an interesting history.

7. [1]So Tilden's political party challenged the electoral college's vote count. [2]Rutherford B. Hayes beat Samuel Tilden by only one electoral vote. [3]Congress had to appoint a special commission to decide on the winner. [4]The election of 1876 was the closest presidential race in U.S. history.

Which arrangement of the sentences would make the best paragraph?

Ⓐ 4 – 2 – 1 – 3   Ⓒ 4 – 1 – 2 – 3
Ⓑ 2 – 1 – 3 – 4   Ⓓ 2 – 4 – 1 – 3

8. [1]Satchel Paige was one of the greatest pitchers ever to play baseball. [2]After the major leagues were integrated in 1947, Paige joined the Cleveland Indians. [3]However, for almost 30 years he was not allowed to play in the major leagues because he was black. [4]His pitching helped Cleveland win the American League championship in 1948.

Which arrangement of the sentences would make the best paragraph?

Ⓐ 1 – 2 – 3 – 4   Ⓒ 1 – 4 – 2 – 3
Ⓑ 1 – 3 – 2 – 4   Ⓓ 1 – 3 – 4 – 2

STOP

Number Correct/Total = _____ /8

Spelling
Recognizing correct spelling

Directions: Choose the correct spelling of the word.

A Lee's moment of _____ cost him the race.

  Ⓐ hesitation

  Ⓑ hestitashen

  Ⓒ hesitatetion

  Ⓓ hesitasion

Directions: Read the phrases. In one of the phrases, the underlined word is spelled incorrectly for the way it is used. Choose the phrase in which the underlined word is NOT spelled correctly.

B Ⓐ those <u>two</u> boxes

  Ⓑ a <u>heard</u> of cows

  Ⓒ <u>dyed</u> hair

  Ⓓ <u>peel</u> a potato

Example A asks you to choose the correct spelling of *hesitation*. Choice Ⓐ is correct. The other choices illustrate some **common spelling errors**.

Example B tests your knowledge of words that sound alike but have different spellings. These words are called **homonyms**, or **homophones**. Some **homophones** are different parts of speech, as in *bear* and *bare*.

Each underlined word in Example B is a real word, but one of them is spelled incorrectly for the way it is used. A group of cows is a *herd*, not a *heard*, so choice Ⓑ is the correct answer.

Here are some general spelling rules you can practice. When you're not sure how to spell a word in your writing, look it up in a dictionary.

Language Rules

▶ Change *y* to *i* before adding an ending that begins with *e*.

  hurry + ed = hurr**ied**
  hurry + es = hurr**ies**

▶ In most one-syllable words ending in one vowel and one consonant, double the consonant before adding an ending.

  swim + er = swi**mm**er
  chat + ing = cha**tt**ing

▶ Use *i* before *e*, except after *c* and in words with the long *a* sound. (Exceptions: n**ei**ther, s**ei**ze, w**ei**rd)

  rel**ie**ve, rec**ei**ve
  n**ei**ghbor, sl**ei**gh

Test-Taking Tips

1 First, eliminate the answers you *know* are misspelled. (Be alert for common spelling errors, such as *hesitasion* vs. *hesitation*.) If you are not sure how a word is spelled, look for the answer choice that looks most familiar.

2 Be careful of questions like Example B, where you are looking for the *incorrect* spelling.

3 In items testing homonyms, look for the correct part of speech.

Go for it

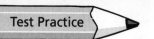

Test Practice 5: Spelling

Time: **18** minutes

Questions 1–18. Choose the word that is spelled correctly.

1. "What an _____ idea!" exclaimed Luis.
   - Ⓐ absurd
   - Ⓑ abserd
   - Ⓒ absird
   - Ⓓ absurred

2. Tanya blushed _____ at my compliments.
   - Ⓐ noticably
   - Ⓑ noticeably
   - Ⓒ noticeabley
   - Ⓓ noticabley

3. Lori wrote the date on her _____.
   - Ⓐ calender
   - Ⓑ callendar
   - Ⓒ calendar
   - Ⓓ calander

4. Dairy products need _____
   - Ⓐ refrigeratian
   - Ⓑ refrigerateion
   - Ⓒ refrigration
   - Ⓓ refrigeration

5. _____ to music is a fun way to keep fit.
   - Ⓐ Exercising
   - Ⓑ Exercizing
   - Ⓒ Exersizing
   - Ⓓ Excercising

6. By _____, they both arrived at noon.
   - Ⓐ coincidents
   - Ⓑ coincidence
   - Ⓒ coinsidense
   - Ⓓ coincidense

7. Jim Henry is so _____.
   - Ⓐ concieted
   - Ⓑ conceated
   - Ⓒ conceited
   - Ⓓ conceted

8. My brother has an _____ friend.
   - Ⓐ imagineary
   - Ⓑ imaginery
   - Ⓒ imageinary
   - Ⓓ imaginary

9. Five of our state _____ met today.
   - Ⓐ representatives
   - Ⓑ representives
   - Ⓒ represenatives
   - Ⓓ repersentatives

10. Jared was _____ sorry.
    - Ⓐ truely
    - Ⓑ trully
    - Ⓒ truley
    - Ⓓ truly

11. She solved the problem _____
    - Ⓐ logicly
    - Ⓑ logically
    - Ⓒ logicaly
    - Ⓓ logickly

12. We roasted three _____
    - Ⓐ turkies
    - Ⓑ turkeies
    - Ⓒ turkeys
    - Ⓓ turkyes

13. He _____ every one of his stories.
    - Ⓐ exagerrates
    - Ⓑ exaggerates
    - Ⓒ exagerates
    - Ⓓ exaggerrates

14. Marilyn has a _____ for you.
    - Ⓐ surprise
    - Ⓑ serprise
    - Ⓒ surprize
    - Ⓓ serprize

15. _____ the carrots and the celery.
    - Ⓐ Seperate
    - Ⓑ Seprate
    - Ⓒ Sepparate
    - Ⓓ Separate

16. Melvin was so _____.
    - Ⓐ embarassed
    - Ⓑ embarrased
    - Ⓒ embarrassed
    - Ⓓ emberrassed

17. Have you ever been to a _____ country?
    - Ⓐ foreign
    - Ⓑ foregn
    - Ⓒ forign
    - Ⓓ forein

18. Night is the _____ of day.
    - Ⓐ oppisite
    - Ⓑ oposite
    - Ⓒ opposite
    - Ⓓ opisite

GO ON ⇨

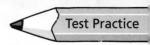

Questions 19–30. Read the phrases. In one of the phrases, the underlined word is spelled incorrectly for the way it is used. Choose the phrase in which the underlined word is NOT spelled correctly.

19. Ⓐ to <u>soar</u> like a bird
    Ⓑ <u>bussed</u> to school
    Ⓒ a construction <u>cite</u>
    Ⓓ <u>heir</u> to the throne

20. Ⓐ the <u>scent</u> of lilacs
    Ⓑ <u>rung</u> out the wet towel
    Ⓒ don't <u>meddle</u> in there
    Ⓓ to <u>hire</u> some help

21. Ⓐ to act on <u>principle</u>
    Ⓑ early morning <u>mist</u>
    Ⓒ the bell <u>tolled</u>
    Ⓓ a bowl of <u>chilly</u>

22. Ⓐ to give wise <u>counsel</u>
    Ⓑ religious <u>rites</u>
    Ⓒ the horse's <u>rains</u>
    Ⓓ a country <u>fair</u>

23. Ⓐ have <u>disgust</u> the matter
    Ⓑ a <u>wry</u> smile
    Ⓒ new <u>cookware</u>
    Ⓓ an alternate <u>route</u>

24. Ⓐ a <u>feat</u> of heroism
    Ⓑ the first <u>seen</u> of the play
    Ⓒ the ship's <u>mast</u>
    Ⓓ a yellow <u>gourd</u>

25. Ⓐ mend a <u>seam</u>
    Ⓑ the actor's <u>role</u>
    Ⓒ <u>shoo</u> away the bugs
    Ⓓ an <u>idol</u> boy

26. Ⓐ a <u>fond</u> look
    Ⓑ fish in the <u>creek</u>
    Ⓒ her <u>bridle</u> gown
    Ⓓ <u>tow</u> a barge

27. Ⓐ a <u>knot</u> in the wood
    Ⓑ to remain <u>stationery</u>
    Ⓒ <u>passed</u> the test
    Ⓓ a <u>lone</u> traveler

28. Ⓐ bus <u>fare</u>
    Ⓑ <u>mints</u> up some garlic
    Ⓒ have a <u>merry</u> time
    Ⓓ a three-<u>course</u> meal

29. Ⓐ <u>heel</u> of a shoe
    Ⓑ <u>peer</u> through the window
    Ⓒ a loaf of <u>bred</u>
    Ⓓ designer <u>clothes</u>

30. Ⓐ sleep in the lower <u>birth</u>
    Ⓑ have <u>banned</u> the movie
    Ⓒ a delicious <u>pear</u>
    Ⓓ <u>buries</u> the treasure

Number Correct/Total = _____ /30

Punctuation

Using correct punctuation in sentences and letters

Directions: Read the letter below. Choose the correct word or group of words for each blank.

> **A**
>
> I am having a party on **B** from 7–10 P.M. If your parents will bring you to my house, my parents will take you home. Please let me know if you can come.
>   Your friend,
>   Allison

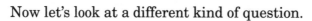

A
Ⓐ Dear Janice
Ⓑ Dear Janice—
Ⓒ Dear Janice;
Ⓓ Dear Janice,

B
Ⓐ Oct 16
Ⓑ Oct. 16
Ⓒ Oct, 16
Ⓓ Oct: 16

This is a friendly letter. A comma is the correct punctuation mark to use after the salutation (greeting) in a friendly letter. So, in Example A, choice Ⓓ is the correct answer.

Example B involves an abbreviation. Since an abbreviation should always end with a period, choice Ⓑ, *Oct. 16*, is correct.

Now let's look at a different kind of question.

Directions: Read each group of sentences. Choose the sentence that uses correct punctuation.

C
Ⓐ By the way, do you know Jackie Lawson?
Ⓑ Of course, I do he's my cousin.
Ⓒ He is on the football team but he's injured.
Ⓓ However; he is about to move to Florida.

D
Ⓐ "I haven't seen her in ages, said Sherry."
Ⓑ "I know", Jean replied.
Ⓒ "Why don't we meet for lunch?" Sherry asked.
Ⓓ "Maybe tomorrow, said Jean, if that's okay with you."

Example C tests the use of commas. Choice Ⓐ is correct because there should be a comma after the introductory phrase (*By the way*). Choice Ⓑ is incorrect because the comma should be after the word *do*. Choice Ⓒ should have a comma after the word *team*. Choice Ⓓ should have a comma instead of a semi-colon after the word *however*.

Example D tests the use of quotation marks. A direct quotation should be enclosed by quotation marks. Choice Ⓒ is correct. In choices Ⓐ and Ⓑ, the closing quotation mark should be after the comma. In choice Ⓓ, there should be a quotation mark after *tomorrow*, and before *if*.

Language Rules

Use a **comma** —

▶ between city and state
> Valdosta, Georgia

▶ between the day and year in a date
> June 16, 1990

▶ to separate items in a series
> He bought books, note paper, and pens.

▶ before the conjunction in a compound sentence
> Mario went to the mall, but he didn't buy anything.

▶ to set off a direct quotation
> "Come on over," said Lou.

▶ after the salutation in a friendly letter and after the closing
> Dear Sarah,
> Forever yours,

▶ to set off introductory words and phrases, appositives, parenthetical phrases, and words of direct address
> In the last week of May, we went fishing at Nag's Head.
> Jonathan, please come in.

Use a **period** —

▶ at the end of declarative and imperative sentences
> The sky is blue.
> Please get some milk.

▶ in abbreviations (except in the names of certain organizations, such as FBI and UNICEF)
> Nov. 16   Mr. Bojangles   10 P.M.

Use an **apostrophe** —

▶ in possessive nouns
> Teddy's bike

▶ in contractions
> He wasn't home.

Use **quotation marks** —

▶ to set off direct quotations
> "Hello, Jake," said Meg.

▶ for the title of a short work (poem, essay, short story, song, etc.)
> "Fire and Ice"
> "That Girl"

Use a **semi-colon** —

▶ between two independent clauses not joined by a conjunction
> Maine and Vermont have cold winters; Vermont has great skiing.

Use a **colon** —

▶ after the salutation in a business letter
> Dear Sirs:

▶ before a list
> Three countries form the Benelux nations: Belgium, the Netherlands, and Luxembourg.

Test-Taking Tips

1 Read each sentence to yourself to see if it sounds right. Wherever you pause in the sentence, there should be a punctuation mark.

2 Look for sentences with missing punctuation.

3 If the sentence has punctuation marks, make sure they are right.

Go for it

Test Practice 6: Punctuation

Time: **12** minutes

Questions 1–8. Read the letter below. Choose the word or phrase with correct punctuation to fit each numbered blank.

Three Island State Park
_____(1)_____

June 14, 1990

_____(2)_____

I am writing this letter at the picnic table in our campground on the banks of the Snake River. _____(3)_____. The cliffs on the other side of the river look as if they have been painted. I can see birds darting around, probably trying to catch the evening bugs. (Ow! A bug just caught *me*!) It's a beautiful spot, _____(4)_____ except for the train that went by about a half hour ago.

Today we visited Craters of the Moon National Monument. _____(5)_____ The entire landscape is made up of _____(6)_____ craters, cinder cones, lava flows, and others. It does seem like the moon, except for the plants and animals that somehow manage to live there.

It is getting too dark to write; I guess I'll go to bed. _____(7)_____ the sleeping bag you gave me was the perfect birthday gift. I have been putting it to good use on this trip.

_____(8)_____
Terrell

---

1. Ⓐ Glenns Ferry Idaho
   Ⓑ Glenns Ferry; Idaho
   Ⓒ Glenns Ferry, Idaho
   Ⓓ Glenns Ferry. Idaho

2. Ⓐ Dear Mrs. Hubbard,
   Ⓑ Dear Mrs Hubbard,
   Ⓒ Dear Mrs, Hubbard,
   Ⓓ Dear Mrs. Hubbard:

3. Ⓐ It is still light out, but the sun is getting low.
   Ⓑ It is still light out; but the sun is getting low.
   Ⓒ It is still light out. But the sun is getting low.
   Ⓓ It is still light out but the sun is getting low.

4. Ⓐ and, extremely quiet too
   Ⓑ and extremely quiet, too,
   Ⓒ and extremely quiet, too;
   Ⓓ and, extremely quiet, too,

5. Ⓐ What a fascinating place.
   Ⓑ What, a fascinating place?
   Ⓒ What a fascinating place;
   Ⓓ What a fascinating place!

6. Ⓐ volcanic features
   Ⓑ volcanic features;
   Ⓒ volcanic features:
   Ⓓ volcanic features—

7. Ⓐ By the way.
   Ⓑ By the way!
   Ⓒ By the way:
   Ⓓ By the way,

8. Ⓐ Yours truly,
   Ⓑ Yours, truly,
   Ⓒ Yours truly:
   Ⓓ Yours truly—

GO ON

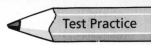

Questions 9–15. Read each group of sentences. Choose the sentence that is punctuated correctly.

9. Ⓐ "Give me liberty, or give me death!," declared Patrick Henry.
   Ⓑ "Thomas Jefferson stated, All men are created equal."
   Ⓒ George Washington wrote, "Liberty, when it begins to take root, is a plant of rapid growth."
   Ⓓ Who said, These are the times that try men's souls?

10. Ⓐ "Jenny, will you answer the telephone, please?"
    Ⓑ "It's for you Mom; shall I take a message?"
    Ⓒ "My mother can't come to the phone, Ms. Daly she'll call you back."
    Ⓓ "Never mind Jenny tell your mother I'll call her another time."

11. Ⓐ A dog was found wandering near Route 4 a busy and dangerous road.
    Ⓑ The dog, a well-groomed Scottish terrier had no collar.
    Ⓒ The dog officer Dana Costanza tried to find out whose dog it was.
    Ⓓ The owners, a family with three small children, could not be found.

12. Ⓐ Senator Boynton didnt vote for the Clean Water bill.
    Ⓑ A reporter asked for the senator's reasons.
    Ⓒ Boynton replied that she did'n't think the bill was strong enough.
    Ⓓ She said that Americas' rivers needed even greater protection.

13. Ⓐ "Some Haystacks Don't Even Have a Needle" is the title of a book of poems.
    Ⓑ The first poem in the book is "An Easy Decision" by Kenneth Patchen.
    Ⓒ The book was reviewed favorably in an essay entitled *Finding the Needle at Last.*
    Ⓓ The essay appeared in "Poetry Today," a magazine devoted to modern poetry.

14. Ⓐ E.M. Forster was a novelist, essayist, and, literary critic.
    Ⓑ His best novel is considered to be: *A Passage to India.*
    Ⓒ He wrote five other novels: *Howards End, Where Angels Fear to Tread, The Longest Journey, A Room with a View,* and *Maurice.*
    Ⓓ Forster belonged to the Bloomsbury Group," whose members also included Virginia Woolf and TS Eliot.

15. Ⓐ Carl is not taking French again next year he is taking Spanish.
    Ⓑ He wants to be a teacher; and thinks that Spanish will be useful.
    Ⓒ Spanish is spoken by more people than any other language except English, Hindi, and Mandarin Chinese.
    Ⓓ Carls knowledge of French should help him learn Spanish because the two languages are similar in many ways.

Number Correct/Total = _____ /15

Capitalization

Using correct capitalization in sentences and letters

Directions: Choose the word or phrase with correct capitalization to complete the sentence.

A The doctor's office is on _____.

   Ⓐ park road
   Ⓑ park Road
   Ⓒ Park road
   Ⓓ Park Road

Directions: Read the sentences. Choose the one that uses correct capitalization.

B Ⓐ Eric's family went to see *The taming of the shrew.*

   Ⓑ The play was at the rainbow theater.

   Ⓒ The lead parts were played by Celia Harris and Richard Aguayo.

   Ⓓ Eric later read a review of the play in *drama.*

In Example A, both words in the street name should be capitalized, so the correct response is Ⓓ. The answer choices in Example B involve names of people, names of buildings, and titles. Choice Ⓒ is the correct response. In Ⓐ and Ⓓ, the important words in the titles should be capitalized; in Ⓑ, the name of the theater should be written *Rainbow Theater.*

Language Rules

▶ Capitalize "firsts"—the first word in a sentence, in a quotation, in a title, in the salutation and closing of a letter.

   "Don't go, Maggie!" he cried.

   Sincerely yours,

▶ Capitalize the names and titles of specific people,

places, and things (but not when used more generally).

   Elm Street, a busy street
   Lake Superior, a clear lake

▶ Capitalize important words in dates, holidays, and addresses.

   the Fourth of July

▶ Capitalize every important word in the title of a song,

story, play, book, or movie.

   "Material Girl"
   Predator

▶ Capitalize proper nouns and proper adjectives which refer to ethnic groups, nationalities, languages, political organizations, businesses and corporations, and religions.

   French-Canadian citizens
   German language
   a Republican mayor

Test-Taking Tips

1 Don't be fooled by answer choices that look almost exactly the same. Check each answer choice carefully, looking for errors in capitalization.

2 If you are not sure which answer choice is correct, choose the one with the most capital letters. It will usually—but not always—be the correct choice.

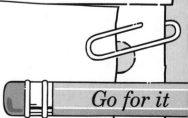

Go for it

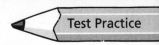

Test Practice 7: Capitalization

Time: **15** minutes

Questions 1–12. Choose the word or phrase with correct capitalization to complete each sentence.

1. _____ and I enjoy roller skating.

   Ⓐ My Friend Sasha
   Ⓑ my friend Sasha
   Ⓒ My friend Sasha
   Ⓓ My friend sasha

2. They went to hear _____ speak about her new book.

   Ⓐ the professor
   Ⓑ The Professor
   Ⓒ The professor
   Ⓓ the Professor

3. The baby was born on _____ .

   Ⓐ Saturday, August 8
   Ⓑ saturday, august 8
   Ⓒ saturday, August 8
   Ⓓ Saturday, august 8

4. The letter was postmarked _____ .

   Ⓐ Madison, South dakota
   Ⓑ Madison, South Dakota
   Ⓒ Madison, south Dakota
   Ⓓ madison, South Dakota

5. Waving her arms, Jackie yelled, _____

   Ⓐ "Look Out for the Car!"
   Ⓑ "look out for the car!"
   Ⓒ "look out for the Car!"
   Ⓓ "Look out for the car!"

6. _____ were at war with each other from 1337 to 1453.

   Ⓐ The french and the english
   Ⓑ The French and The English
   Ⓒ the French and the English
   Ⓓ The French and the English

7. The school is holding an all-night dance on _____

   Ⓐ New year's eve
   Ⓑ New Year's Eve
   Ⓒ New Year's eve
   Ⓓ New year's Eve

8. President Kennedy founded the _____ in 1961.

   Ⓐ Peace corps
   Ⓑ Peace Corps
   Ⓒ peace corps
   Ⓓ peace Corps

9. Chen is fluent in both _____.

   Ⓐ japanese and Russian
   Ⓑ Japanese and russian
   Ⓒ Japanese and Russian
   Ⓓ japanese and russian

10. The story was called _____

    Ⓐ "The Name of the Game."
    Ⓑ "the Name of the Game."
    Ⓒ "The Name Of The Game."
    Ⓓ The name of the game."

11. The hikers soon reached the top of _____

    Ⓐ south Eagle mountain
    Ⓑ South Eagle mountain
    Ⓒ South Eagle Mountain
    Ⓓ south Eagle Mountain

12. Which is the correct way to end a letter?

    Ⓐ As Always,
    Ⓑ as always,
    Ⓒ as Always,
    Ⓓ As always,

GO ON

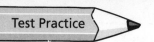

Questions 13–20. In each group of sentences, choose the one that uses correct capitalization.

13. Ⓐ The Democratic candidate was Mayor of the state's largest city.
    Ⓑ His opponent had been Governor for eight years.
    Ⓒ His campaign was helped by an endorsement from Senator Gomez.
    Ⓓ The President of the Police Association backed the other party.

14. Ⓐ On May Third, I am going on an architectural tour of Granville.
    Ⓑ We will see the Stolsky Building, the Gennaro museum, and City College's new Library.
    Ⓒ The new bank building at 1 Manhattan place has an unusual design.
    Ⓓ The tour begins at the Benson County Historical Society.

15. Ⓐ Scholars believe that the nursery rhyme "little Jack Horner" is based on an actual incident in sixteenth-century England.
    Ⓑ The abbot of Glastonbury sent King Henry VIII an unusual gift, a pie containing the deeds to some valuable property.
    Ⓒ The poem says, "he stuck in his thumb and pulled out a plum."
    Ⓓ The abbot's steward, thomas horner, is said to have kept one of the deeds — a "plum" — for himself.

16. Ⓐ The amused Zookeeper opened the letter and began to read aloud.
    Ⓑ The computer-generated letter began, "dear Ms. Panda."
    Ⓒ "We at the Vernon Savings bank are pleased to send you the enclosed credit card."
    Ⓓ "Well," said the keeper to the giant panda in a nearby pen, "Shall we go buy you some bamboo?"

17. Ⓐ The first observance of Arbor Day took place in Nebraska.
    Ⓑ On april 10, 1872, Nebraskans planted over a million trees.
    Ⓒ Other States soon took up the idea of a tree-planting day.
    Ⓓ Today the Holiday is celebrated in most States, and in Canada, too.

18. Ⓐ at 8.9 kilometers, Mount Everest is the highest peak in the world.
    Ⓑ The first people to reach the top, in 1953, were tenzing norgay and Edmund Hillary.
    Ⓒ Norgay was a member of the sherpas, a group of people living high in the mountains of Nepal.
    Ⓓ Hillary, originally a beekeeper, was from New Zealand.

19. Ⓐ The Klein Family has a foreign student living with them this year.
    Ⓑ Pieter Martens comes from the small belgian town of Temse.
    Ⓒ He likes to joke that his favorite vegetable is Brussels sprouts.
    Ⓓ Then he always explains, "our capital is Brussels, you know."

20. Ⓐ Do you want to go camping at the Lake this weekend?
    Ⓑ *The Guidebook to Great Camping* gives the campground a good rating.
    Ⓒ The National Park service charges a fee of five dollars per tent.
    Ⓓ We plan to leave early Saturday Morning.

STOP

Number Correct/Total = _____ /20

Research Skills

Completing outlines to organize information

Directions: Use the outline to answer each question.

I. Types and Uses of Plastics
   A. _____
   B. Medical Uses
   C. Household Uses
   D. Recreational Uses
II. History of Plastics
   A. Forerunners to Plastics
   B. Development of Plastics
   C. Today's Plastics Industry

A Which subheading would best fit in the blank at I A?

Ⓐ Early Forms of Plastics
Ⓑ Industrial Uses
Ⓒ Leading Plastics Manufacturers
Ⓓ Uses by Hospitals

B Information about plastic sports equipment belongs in which section?

Ⓐ I B   Ⓒ I D
Ⓑ I C   Ⓓ II B

In Example A, you must choose the answer that best fits the blank in the outline. The blank appears under the heading "Types and Uses of Plastics." Two of the answer choices, Ⓑ and Ⓓ, have to do with uses of plastics.

Choice Ⓓ belongs as a topic under "Medical Uses"; the correct response is Ⓑ, *Industrial Uses*.

Questions such as Example B ask you to find the best place in the outline for a certain topic or piece of information. In this case, the best answer is choice Ⓒ, I D, *Recreational Uses*, because sports equipment is an example of a recreational use of plastics.

Most outlines use the same grammatical form in each section (sentences, words, or phrases). **Main headings** are the most general; they are labeled with Roman numerals (I, II, III, etc.). **Subheadings** (A, B, C, etc.) are listed under the main headings. Some outlines also have numbered **topics** (1, 2, 3, etc.) and **subtopics** (a, b, c, etc.).

Hint

You can use outlining in your schoolwork. When you read, organize your notes in outline form to help you remember what you have read. When you write, use an outline to plan your work; then the writing will be easier.

Test-Taking Tips

1 Look for information that fits within the main heading of each section.

2 When filling a blank in the outline, look for the answer that is in the same grammatical form as the rest of the outline. (*Industrial Uses* has the same form as *Medical Uses*.)

Go for it

Test Practice 8: Research Skills

Time: **8** minutes

Directions: Use the outline to answer each question.

Dwight D. Eisenhower (1890–1969)

I. Early Life
    A. _____
    B. Boyhood

II. Military Career
     A. Early Years
     B. World War II
        1. War Department
        2. Europe
        3. Africa
     C. NATO Commander

III. Post-War Period (1945–1952)
      A. Family Life
      B. Columbia University President

IV. The Republican Party

V. President of the U.S.
    A. First Administration (1953–57)
       1. Election of 1952
       2. Foreign Affairs
       3. Domestic Affairs
       4. Major Accomplishments
    B. Second Administration (1957–61)
       1. Election of 1956
       2. Foreign Affairs
       3. Domestic Affairs
       4. _____

VI. Final Years

---

1. This outline would be most useful for planning a —

    ⓐ biography of Eisenhower
    ⓑ comparison of the Truman and Eisenhower presidencies
    ⓒ report about World War II
    ⓓ report about Eisenhower's role in the Korean War

2. Which subheading best fits in the blank at I A?

    ⓐ War College
    ⓑ Family
    ⓒ Major Battles
    ⓓ Elections

3. Information about Eisenhower's education should be included in which section?

    ⓐ I B
    ⓑ II A
    ⓒ III B
    ⓓ VI

4. Which topic would best fit in the blank at V B–4?

    ⓐ U.S.–Soviet Relations
    ⓑ State-of-the-Union address
    ⓒ Retirement at Gettysburg
    ⓓ Major Accomplishments

5. In 1954, Senator Joseph McCarthy accused members of Eisenhower's administration of being communist. This incident would be included in what section of the outline?

    ⓐ V A–1
    ⓑ V A–3
    ⓒ V B–1
    ⓓ V B–3

6. Which heading does NOT belong in this outline?

    ⓐ I.   Early Life
    ⓑ II. Military Career
    ⓒ IV. The Republican Party
    ⓓ V.   President of the U.S.

STOP

Number Correct/Total = _____ /6

Reference Sources

Locating information in reference sources
and parts of books

Directions: Read each question. Choose the correct answer.

A To find out when the Civil War began, you should look in —

Ⓐ an atlas

Ⓑ a newspaper

Ⓒ an encyclopedia

Ⓓ a telephone directory

B In a dictionary, the word *defray* would appear on the same page as which set of guide words?

Ⓐ decoy – deep

Ⓑ deer – defend

Ⓒ defense – defoliate

Ⓓ deform – degree

Example A is a general question about the kinds of information found in different reference sources. The correct answer is Ⓒ because an *encyclopedia* would be the best place to look for the information. A newspaper, choice Ⓑ, would be most useful for finding information about current events and issues. Neither an atlas, choice Ⓐ nor a telephone directory, choice Ⓓ would be a good place to look.

Example B asks how to use a specific reference source. This question has to do with using a dictionary. You have to choose from among four sets of dictionary guide words. **Guide words** are the pairs of words that appear on the top of each page in a dictionary. For this question, the correct answer is Ⓓ, because the word *defray* comes between *deform* and *degree* in alphabetical order. The guide words *deform – degree* would appear on the same dictionary page as the word *defray*.

Other kinds of test questions give you an excerpt from a book or other reference source. Let's look at this example.

INDEX

Board games, 125–140
Card games, 51–68
   bridge, 57–58
   cribbage, 61–62
   poker, 52–54
   solitaire, 59–60
   whist, 65–67
Checkers, 3–5
Chess, 6–11
Darts, 102–106
Dice, 74–83 *See also* **Yahtzee**
Dominoes, 43–45
Mah–jongg, 47–49

Directions: Use this sample index from a book about games to answer each question.

C To find information about dominoes, you should look on pages —

Ⓐ 125–140   Ⓒ 47–49

Ⓑ 102–106   Ⓓ 43–45

D To find more information about dice games, you should look under what topic?

Ⓐ Bridge   Ⓒ Mah-jongg

Ⓑ Yahtzee   Ⓓ Solitaire

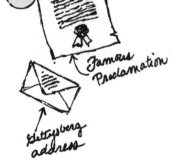

Example C asks on which pages you would find information about dominoes. The correct answer is Ⓓ, *43–45*. If you look in the index under *dominoes*, you will see the page numbers *43–45* beside the topic.

Example D asks where to find more information about dice games. If you look in the index under *dice*, the entry lists some page numbers, 74–83, and says *See also* **Yahtzee**. This is called a **cross-reference**. A cross-reference tells you where you can find more information about the topic you are looking for. The correct answer to the question is choice Ⓑ, *Yahtzee*.

Hints

The list below describes the most widely used reference sources and kinds of information they provide.

▶ **Almanac**
A collection of facts and figures, updated every year.

▶ **Atlas**
A book of maps.

▶ **Bibliography**
A list of references used to write a book or a report.

▶ **Card Catalog**
A card file in the library: it lists every book by author, by subject, and by title, and it tells you where to find the book in the library.

▶ **Dictionary**
Dictionaries are arranged in alphabetical order; they provide definitions of words, pronunciation, syllables, and etymologies, or word histories.

▶ **Encyclopedia**
A collection of short articles on a wide range of topics. Most encyclopedias are arranged in volumes, in alphabetical order.

▶ **Glossary**
Like a dictionary, but the glossary appears in the back of a book. It gives definitions for special words used in the book.

▶ **Magazines**
Most magazines come out every month, or every week. They are useful sources of information for news and current events of the last few weeks.

▶ **Newspapers**
Daily newspapers provide the most up-to-date information and news.

▶ *Readers' Guide to Periodical Literature*
A guide to articles which have been published in magazines and journals. This guide is organized by dates, by subject, by title, and by author.

▶ **Telephone Directory**
The "White Pages" list people's names, addresses, and telephone numbers, in alphabetical order. The "Yellow Pages" list names, addresses, and telephone numbers of businesses, arranged mainly by topic.

▶ **Thesaurus**
Similar to a dictionary, this is a word book. It is most useful for finding synonyms for words. It is usually arranged by topic and/or in alphabetical order.

Test-Taking Tips

1 Look for key words to answer each question. (In Example A, the key words are *when* and *Civil War*.)

2 Refer back to the excerpt or sample reference to find the answers. To answer Examples C and D, you should refer back to the sample index given on the page.

Go for it

Test Practice 9: Reference Sources

Time: **12** minutes

Questions 1–4. Choose the best answer to each question.

1. In a report, you have used the word *regulate* eight times and want to substitute some other words that mean the same thing. The best reference source would be a —

   Ⓐ dictionary
   Ⓑ thesaurus
   Ⓒ glossary
   Ⓓ bibliography

2. If you wanted to find the names of major rivers in the nation of Botswana, which would be the best place to look?

   Ⓐ an atlas
   Ⓑ a travel magazine
   Ⓒ an index
   Ⓓ a card catalog

3. You are writing a report on modern Utah, and you want to find some recent magazine articles about Utah. Which would be the best reference source?

   Ⓐ encyclopedia
   Ⓑ bibliography
   Ⓒ thesaurus
   Ⓓ *Readers' Guide to Periodical Literature*

4. If you wanted to find information about motion pictures directed by D.W. Griffith, in which volume of the encyclopedia should you look?

   Ⓐ Volume 3: D–E
   Ⓑ Volume 6: G–H
   Ⓒ Volume 9: M
   Ⓓ Volume 11: P

Questions 5–8. Use the sample dictionary entries to answer the questions.

---

cai·man (kā′ mə n) *n.* an aquatic reptile of South and Central America, closely related to the alligator. [Sp. *caiman* < Carib native word]

ca·ique (kä ēk′) *n.* 1. a long narrow rowboat, popular in Turkey. 2. a sailboat used in the eastern Mediterranean. [Fr. *caique* < It. *caicco* < Turk. qayiq, boat]

cairn (kârn) *n.* a mound of stones built as a monument or landmark. [Gaelic *carn*, heap of stones]

---

5. What is a *cairn*?

   Ⓐ an alligator-like reptile
   Ⓑ a building
   Ⓒ a pile of stones
   Ⓓ a type of boat

6. What part of speech is the word *caiman*?

   Ⓐ adjective
   Ⓑ adverb
   Ⓒ noun
   Ⓓ verb

7. The word *caique* comes originally from what language?

   Ⓐ Spanish
   Ⓑ French
   Ⓒ Italian
   Ⓓ Turkish

8. Which guide words would appear on this dictionary page?

   Ⓐ cadet – Caesar
   Ⓑ caftan – Cajun
   Ⓒ cake – calcite

Questions 9–11. Use this sample index to answer each question.

INDEX

Tadpoles, 119
Terrapin, 37
Texas Rattler, 111
Timber Rattler, 111–112
Toads, 116–123
    American, 122–123
    Bell, 120
    Great Plains, 123
    Spadefoot, 121
    Western, 123
    See also **Tadpoles**
Tortoise, 27
Tree Frogs, 126–128
Turtles, 18–43
    Box, 18, 38–39
    Green, 19, 21
    Leatherback, 19, 20–21
    Mud, 19, 23
    Painted, 32–33
    Snappers, 19, 24–25
    See also **Terrapin**, **Tortoise**

9. To find information about painted turtles, you should look on pages —
   - Ⓐ 20–21
   - Ⓑ 24–25
   - Ⓒ 32–33
   - Ⓓ 38–39

10. Information about tree frogs would be found on pages —
   - Ⓐ 18–43
   - Ⓑ 116–119
   - Ⓒ 122–123
   - Ⓓ 126–128

11. To find additional information about toads, you should look under —
   - Ⓐ Frogs
   - Ⓑ Tadpoles
   - Ⓒ Tortoise
   - Ⓓ Terrapin

Questions 12–15. Use this sample catalog card to answer each question.

598.1
T   **Tenny, Myra S.**, 1937–

    Reptiles and amphibians; a guide to American species, by Myra S. Tenny; illus. by Barry Linfield. Science Books 1987.

    199 p., illus., maps

    1. Frogs   2. Reptiles   I. Title

12. When was this book published?
   - Ⓐ 1937
   - Ⓑ 1958
   - Ⓒ 1987
   - Ⓓ 1990

13. What is the title of this book?
   - Ⓐ Tenny, Myra S.
   - Ⓑ Frogs
   - Ⓒ A Guide to American Species
   - Ⓓ Reptiles and Amphibians

14. Who illustrated this book?
   - Ⓐ Barry Linfield
   - Ⓑ Science Books
   - Ⓒ Myra S. Tenny
   - Ⓓ American Species

15. What is the Dewey Decimal number for this book?
   - Ⓐ 1937–
   - Ⓑ 199 p
   - Ⓒ 598.1
   - Ⓓ 1987

STOP

Number Correct/Total = _____ /15

Maps, Charts, and Graphs

Interpreting data from graphic aids

Directions: Some students at the Monroe Middle School took a survey of their classmates to help them plan an end-of-year celebration. Use the table of their survey results to answer the questions.

PREFERRED ACTIVITY				
Grade	Cookout	Dance Party	Field Trip	Talent Show
5	22	8	15	10
6	24	10	17	10
7	20	20	6	3
8	24	30	10	0
Total	90	68	48	23

A Which activity was preferred by the most sixth graders?

Ⓐ cookout
Ⓑ dance party
Ⓒ field trip
Ⓓ talent show

B What conclusion can be drawn from the information in this table?

Ⓐ Talent shows are popular among the eighth graders.
Ⓑ The older students are more interested in cookouts than the younger students are.
Ⓒ Field trips are the most popular activity in every grade.
Ⓓ The fifth and sixth graders in this school have similar preferences.

Test questions like these ask you to find and interpret information in charts and tables, graphs, schedules, advertisements, and maps. The answer to Example A is in the table. Find the row for Grade 6 responses to the survey. Then look for the largest number. The correct answer is Ⓐ, *cookout*, because 24 students chose this activity. Fewer students chose each of the other activities.

Example B asks you to draw a conclusion from the information in the table. The best way to approach this question is to look at each of the answer choices. Then refer back to the table to see if the information supports, or does not support, each of the answer choices. Choice Ⓓ is the correct answer. You can see that the preferences among the fifth and sixth graders are quite similar by looking at the numbers in each column; they are almost the same. The information in the table does not support any of the other answer choices.

Test-Taking Tips

1 Look for key words and phrases to answer the questions. (In Example A, the key words are *most sixth graders*.)

2 To draw conclusions, look at each of the answer choices. Try to find information that supports, or does not support, each of the choices.

Go for it

Test Practice 10 : Maps, Charts, and Graphs   Time: 10 minutes

Questions 1–6. Use the advertisement and schedule below to answer each question.

WESTWIND WHALE WATCHING
"The Greatest Show on Earth"

Featuring Humpback whales
Finback whales
Right whales
Minke whales

- Sail with Westwind's experienced crews.
- In 1989, our passengers sighted whales on more than 99% of our cruises!
- Bring camera, rubber-soled shoes, sunglasses, jacket.
- Food & beverages available on board.

Six cruises daily from the
South Pier at Cutter's Point.

Rates: Adults $12
        Children under 16 $6

WESTWIND WHALE WATCHING
Summer Schedule

Boat	Mon–Fri		Sat/Sun/Holiday	
	Leave	Return	Leave	Return
The Westerly				
	8:30 A.M.	1:00 A.M.	8:30 A.M.	1:00 A.M.
	2:30 A.M.	7:00 P.M.	2:30 P.M.	7:00 P.M.
The New Bedford				
	9:15 A.M.	11:00 A.M.	11:00 A.M.	3:30 P.M.
	3:00 P.M.	7:30 P.M.	5:00 P.M.	9:30 P.M.
The Cape Ann				
	10:00 A.M.	2:30 P.M.		

Call for information: (504) 555-1900

1. How many different kinds of whales can be seen on the Westwind cruise?

   Ⓐ 4   Ⓒ 12
   Ⓑ 6   Ⓓ 16

2. At what time does The Cape Ann return from its cruise on Monday–Friday?

   Ⓐ 1:00 P.M.   Ⓒ 3:30 P.M.
   Ⓑ 2:30 P.M.   Ⓓ 10:00 A.M.

3. All of the Westwind cruises leave from —

   Ⓐ Cape Ann   Ⓒ Cutter's Point
   Ⓑ New Bedford   Ⓓ Westerly

4. The advertisement and the schedule disagree on the —

   Ⓐ number of cruises per day
   Ⓑ departure times
   Ⓒ telephone number for information
   Ⓓ ticket prices

5. At what time does the last cruise leave on Tuesdays in the summer?

   Ⓐ 10:00 A.M.   Ⓒ 3:00 P.M.
   Ⓑ   2:30 P.M.   Ⓓ 7:30 P.M.

6. Which part of the advertisement would be most useful for deciding whether to choose Westwind or another whale-watching cruise?

   Ⓐ the words "The Greatest Show on Earth"
   Ⓑ the statement that the crew is experienced
   Ⓒ the percentage of whale sightings on cruises in 1989
   Ⓓ the list of things to bring

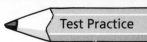

Questions 7–12. Use this map to answer the questions.

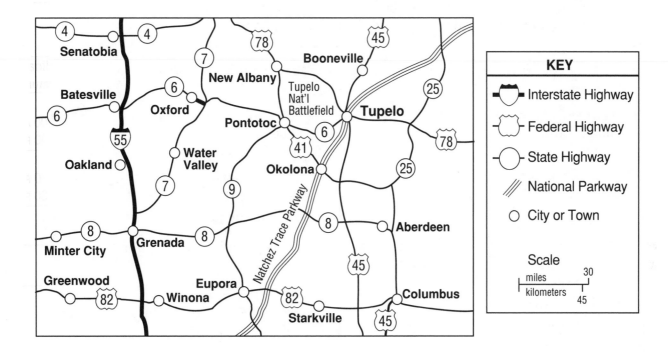

7. If you traveled from Grenada to Oxford, you would be traveling in what direction?

   Ⓐ southeast   Ⓒ southwest
   Ⓑ northeast   Ⓓ northwest

8. Which city lies at the intersection of routes 41 and 6?

   Ⓐ Okolona
   Ⓑ Senatobia
   Ⓒ Batesville
   Ⓓ Pontotoc

9. What type of road is Route 55?

   Ⓐ interstate highway
   Ⓑ state highway
   Ⓒ federal highway
   Ⓓ national parkway

10. If you took Route 82 from Eupora to Columbus, you would pass through —

    Ⓐ Winona   Ⓒ Aberdeen
    Ⓑ Greenwood   Ⓓ Starkville

11. About how far is it from Okolona to Booneville?

    Ⓐ 15 miles   Ⓒ 45 miles
    Ⓑ 30 miles   Ⓓ 60 miles

12. To travel from Minter City to the Tupelo National Battlefield, the best way would be to take —

    Ⓐ Route 8 to Route 9
    Ⓑ Route 7 to Route 4
    Ⓒ Route 8 to Route 55
    Ⓓ Route 55 to Route 82

Number Correct/Total = _____ /12

*This test will tell you how well you might score on a standardized language arts test **after** using this book. If you compare your scores on Tryout Tests 1 and 2, you'll see how much you've learned!*

Language Arts Tryout Test 2

Time: **30** minutes

Directions: Follow the directions for each part of the test. Read each question carefully and fill in the circle for the answer you choose. The answer to the sample question (**S**) has been filled in for you.

Questions 1–5. Choose the word or group of words that belongs in the blank.

S Neither Sharon nor her mother _____ the flat tire.

Ⓐ noticing
Ⓑ have noticed
● noticed
Ⓓ notice

1. Until last year, Elsie _____ her cousin Lydia every summer.

Ⓐ had visited
Ⓑ is visiting
Ⓒ will visit
Ⓓ has visited

2. _____ enjoy going to the mall.

Ⓐ Him and his friends
Ⓑ His friends and him
Ⓒ He and his friends
Ⓓ His friends and he

3. Be sure to rinse the dishes _____ with hot water.

Ⓐ more thorough
Ⓑ thorough
Ⓒ most thoroughly
Ⓓ thoroughly

4. This plum is the _____ of all.

Ⓐ sweetest
Ⓑ sweeter
Ⓒ most sweet
Ⓓ most sweetest

5. _____ Jay's birthday on Friday.

Ⓐ Didn't nobody remember
Ⓑ Nobody remembered
Ⓒ Anybody didn't remember
Ⓓ Nobody didn't remember

Questions 6–8. Read the four groups of words. Choose the one that is a complete sentence written correctly.

6. Ⓐ Horse races at the county fair, which she had never watched before.
   Ⓑ The jockeys' silks reminded her of brightly colored flags.
   Ⓒ The horses leapt from their starting gates their hooves blurred.
   Ⓓ In a very short time, less than two minutes from start to finish.

7. Ⓐ Crack four eggs into a bowl, be sure to remove any pieces of shell.
   Ⓑ Stirring while you slowly add milk, until you have a smooth batter.
   Ⓒ Dip bread into the batter, bread that is a little stale is best.
   Ⓓ Brown the bread on both sides in a hot pan; serve it with syrup.

8. Ⓐ Although he had been away for years, Cy still knew his way around town.
   Ⓑ Looking up at the tall buildings, thinking back to his childhood.
   Ⓒ On the corner where Mr. Shaw's hardware store used to be.
   Ⓓ Down the street was an ice cream shop it was not there when Cy lived in this neighborhood.

GO ON

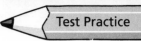

Questions 9–10. Read the underlined sentences. Choose the answer that best combines them into one clear sentence without changing their meaning.

9. I wore a green T-shirt.
   Len wore a green T-shirt.
   Julie wore a green T-shirt.

   Ⓐ Len, Julie, and I wore T-shirts that were the same color.
   Ⓑ I wore a green T-shirt, and so did Len, and so did Julie.
   Ⓒ Len, Julie, and I all wore green T-shirts.
   Ⓓ I wore a green T-shirt, Len and Julie also wore green T-shirts.

10. Paco polished the trumpet.
    The trumpet had belonged to his father.

    Ⓐ Paco polished the trumpet, which had belonged to his father.
    Ⓑ The trumpet belonged to Paco's father, but Paco was polishing it.
    Ⓒ Paco polished his father's trumpet.
    Ⓓ Paco polished the trumpet, it had belonged to his father.

Questions 11–12. Read each paragraph. Then answer the question.

11. _____ They remember being amused by the story as children, or watching a cartoon version, and never realized that these were based on a "real" book. Jonathan Swift's famous novel is often studied as a masterpiece of satire. In describing Gulliver's four voyages, Swift ridiculed everything from scientific experimentation to pious hypocrisy. The result is a thought-provoking, if sometimes disturbing, look at society and human nature.

    Which would be the best topic sentence for the paragraph?

    Ⓐ People usually think of Jonathan Swift in connection with his book *Gulliver's Travels*, but the English author wrote a number of other works as well.
    Ⓑ Good satire must be entertaining, or readers may put the book down before they get the point.
    Ⓒ Movie-goers often forget that behind most good films lies an even better book.
    Ⓓ Many young people are surprised to discover *Gulliver's Travels* on their assigned reading list for school.

12. ¹Lumbering clumsily along the forest floor, the porcupine moved more like a child's wind-up toy than an animal. ²Periodically, it rolled up onto its haunches to examine its surroundings, peering around and sniffing the air. ³Then, apparently satisfied that all was well, it continued on its leisurely way. ⁴Porcupines live in the forest, dining on leaves, tree bark, and anything salty. ⁵They can move quickly when they have to, but this one evidently felt no such need.

    Which sentence does NOT belong in the paragraph?

    Ⓐ 2   Ⓑ 3   Ⓒ 4   Ⓓ 5

Language Arts Tryout Test 2 (continued)

Questions 13–16. Read the phrases. In one of the phrases, the underlined word is spelled incorrectly for the way it is used. Choose the phrase in which the underlined word is NOT spelled correctly.

13. Ⓐ two <u>rows</u> of chairs
    Ⓑ a <u>sore</u> thumb
    Ⓒ mining silver <u>ore</u>
    Ⓓ a freshwater <u>pawned</u>

14. Ⓐ year <u>scents</u> I saw you
    Ⓑ the bride's <u>veil</u>
    Ⓒ a dinner <u>roll</u>
    Ⓓ <u>freeze</u> some ice cream

15. Ⓐ South <u>Sea</u> islands
    Ⓑ ham and cheese on <u>wry</u> bread
    Ⓒ cards and other <u>stationery</u>
    Ⓓ <u>heed</u> a warning

16. Ⓐ five <u>feet</u>, two inches
    Ⓑ after-dinner <u>mints</u>
    Ⓒ drive on <u>Root</u> 116 north
    Ⓓ strumming a <u>lute</u>

Questions 17–22. Read each group of sentences. Choose the sentence that uses correct punctuation and capitalization.

17. Ⓐ The port of Hong Kong is the worlds most densely populated city.
    Ⓑ Over five million people live in an area of only twenty square miles, that is more than 250,000 people per square mile.
    Ⓒ In contrast, New York City has 11,400 people per square mile.
    Ⓓ Housing is scarce in Hong Kong and whole families often share a single room.

18. Ⓐ "Look at me, Pete!" squealed Janine, Pete's little sister.
    Ⓑ Pete looked up from "Treasure Island," his favorite book.
    Ⓒ Janine had a bandanna on her head, and a patch over her left eye.
    Ⓓ Grinning, she asked, "Don't I look like Long john silver?"

19. Ⓐ Should any language but english be used in our public schools?
    Ⓑ Parents scholars and educators hotly debate that question.
    Ⓒ Some fear that children, who speak another language, may fall behind their classmates.
    Ⓓ With lessons conducted in their native language, these children can keep up while they learn their new language.

20. Ⓐ Mr Jann, the mayor, formed a committee to beautify Jakobson Park.
    Ⓑ Several students are on the committee, Sue, Joan, Ken, Ted, and Li.
    Ⓒ Friday May 14 will be Clean-Up Day at the park.
    Ⓓ Li's job is to make posters; Ted's job is to notify the newspaper.

21. Ⓐ The popular tomato was for many years shunned as being poisonous.
    Ⓑ It's botanical family does include several poisonous plants!
    Ⓒ Tomatoes are edible; and are excellent sources of vitamins A and C.
    Ⓓ most home gardeners try to grow at least one variety of tomato.

22. Ⓐ Gridlock is a traffic problem, that sometimes affects large cities.
    Ⓑ It begins when cars going in one direction block an intersection.
    Ⓒ The cross-traffic gets backed up and blocks other streets
    Ⓓ It can take the Police several hours to unravel a gridlock.

GO ON

Questions 23–25. Use the outline to answer each question.

Television

I. History and Development

II. How a Television Set Works

III. How Television Programs are Produced

IV. _____
    A. Commercial Television
    B. Public Television
    C. Cable or Pay Television
    D. Effects on Children

V. Television's Role in U.S. Society
    A. Entertainment
    B. Information
    C. Education
    D. Buying a Television

VI. Government Regulations

---

23. Which heading would best fit in the blank at IV?

Ⓐ Late-Night Television
Ⓑ Types of Programming
Ⓒ Old Movies
Ⓓ Situation Comedies

24. Which subheading belongs under heading III?

Ⓐ The Role of the Director
Ⓑ Early Television Stars
Ⓒ Types of Video Games
Ⓓ Television Around the World

25. Which subheading does NOT belong under V?

Ⓐ A. Entertainment
Ⓑ B. Information
Ⓒ C. Education
Ⓓ D. Buying a Television

Questions 26–29. Use the sample dictionary entries to answer each question.

---

sap·id (săp′ id) *adj.* 1. Having a pleasing taste. 2. Interesting or agreeable to the mind. [L. *sapidus,* having a taste] **sap·id·i·ty** *n.*

sa·pi·ent (sā′ pē ənt) *adj.* wise, knowing, full of knowledge [Middle Eng.< L *sapiens,* from *sapere,* to taste, know] **sa·pi·ence** *n.*

sap·o·na·ceous (săp′ ə nā′ shəs) *adj.* soapy; like soap. [L *sapo,* soap]

sap·phire (săf′ īr) *n.* 1. A clear, deep blue precious stone. 2. Its color. [Ofr *saphir* < L. *sapphirus* < Gr. *sappheiros* < Heb. *sapir* < Sanskrit *śanipriya,* dear to Saturn]

---

26. What does *saponaceous* mean?

Ⓐ full of knowledge
Ⓑ tasty
Ⓒ clear, deep blue
Ⓓ soapy

27. What part of speech is the word *sapid*?

Ⓐ adjective   Ⓒ adverb
Ⓑ noun   Ⓓ verb

28. The word *sapphire* originally came from what language?

Ⓐ Latin   Ⓒ Sanskrit
Ⓑ Greek   Ⓓ Middle English

29. These words would appear on the same dictionary page as which set of guide words?

Ⓐ sandwich – sansei
Ⓑ santur – Saracen
Ⓒ sargassum – sash
Ⓓ sassaby – Saturday

GO ON ⟩

Questions 30–32. Use the map to answer each question.

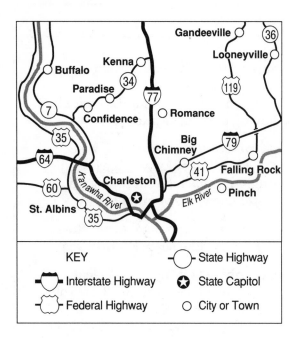

KEY

⬭— State Highway

🖛—Interstate Highway

⭐ State Capitol

〈—Federal Highway

○ City or Town

30. Which route follows the Kanawha River into Charleston?

Ⓐ Route 77   Ⓒ Route 119

Ⓑ Route 35   Ⓓ Route 79

31. What kind of road is Route 64?

Ⓐ city

Ⓑ state

Ⓒ federal highway

Ⓓ interstate highway

32. To get from Big Chimney to Looneyville, you should take —

Ⓐ Route 79 to Route 36

Ⓑ Route 119 to Route 79

Ⓒ Route 77 to Route 34

Ⓓ Route 36 to Route 119

Questions 33–36. Choose the best answer to each question.

33. The best source of information about a local hazardous waste problem would be —

Ⓐ an encyclopedia

Ⓑ a newspaper

Ⓒ *Readers' Guide to Periodical Literature*

Ⓓ an almanac

34. If you wanted to compare the per capita incomes in several states for the year 1990, you should consult —

Ⓐ an almanac

Ⓑ a magazine

Ⓒ an atlas

Ⓓ a bibliography

35. If you wanted to find out what books a library has on political cartoons by Rube Goldberg, you should look in the card catalog under —

Ⓐ cartoons

Ⓑ political

Ⓒ Rube

Ⓓ Goldberg

36. You have just read a book on environmental issues and you want to know what references the author used. You should look in the —

Ⓐ glossary

Ⓑ bibliography

Ⓒ index

Ⓓ table of contents

Number Correct/Total = _____ /36

Math

Top Ten Math Tips

1 Use scratch paper to write down the numbers you need to solve a problem.

2 Look for key words that tell you what kind of computation is needed, for example: *less than, greatest, between, nearest, least, closest,* and so on.

3 Try out *all* answer choices until you find the one that is correct. Sometimes the correct answer is *not given*. Then you should follow the directions for marking the Not Given choice (NG in this book).

4 Make sure you know what to solve for in each problem. Write a number sentence or an equation to help you solve it.

5 Write down each piece of information given in a problem, and write down or circle what each problem asks you to find. When you have an answer, go back and make sure it answers the question you wrote down or circled.

6 Rename fractions with different denominators as *like fractions* (with same denominators).

7 Always reduce fractions to their smallest parts. When looking for the correct answer to a problem with fractions, look for the one that has been reduced.

8 For a measurement or geometry problem, first write down the formula you need to solve the problem. Then "plug into" the formula the numbers from the problem.

9 Remember, an equation must stay balanced. What you do to one side of an equation you must do to the other side.

10 Check subtraction problems by adding; check division problems by multiplying; check multiplication by dividing.

This test will tell you how well you might score on a standardized math test **before** using this book.

Test Practice

Math Tryout Test 1

Time: **40** minutes

Directions: Find the best answer for each question. Fill in the circle beside your answer. If the correct answer is not given, choose NG. The answer to the sample question (**S**) has been filled in for you.

S Which number is 10,000 more than 5,687,312?

Ⓐ 5,787,312

● 5,697,312

Ⓒ 5,688,312

Ⓓ 5,667,312

---

1. $3.75 \times 10^2 = \square$

Ⓐ .375   Ⓒ 375

Ⓑ 37.5   Ⓓ 3750

2. Which is a composite number?

Ⓐ 37   Ⓒ 51

Ⓑ 43   Ⓓ 69

3. What are the prime factors of 30?

Ⓐ $2 \times 3 \times 5$ Ⓒ 15×2

Ⓑ 6×5 Ⓓ 10×3

4. What is the least common multiple of 16 and 12?

Ⓐ 4   Ⓒ 48

Ⓑ 64   Ⓓ 192

5. What is the square root of 81?

Ⓐ 8   Ⓒ 12

Ⓑ 9   Ⓓ 27

6. $-28 + -4 = \square$

Ⓐ 24   Ⓒ −24

Ⓑ 32   Ⓓ −32

7. Which is equal to $3\frac{4}{5}$?

Ⓐ $\frac{7}{5}$ Ⓒ $\frac{19}{5}$

Ⓑ $\frac{12}{5}$ Ⓓ $\frac{12}{15}$

8. What does n stand for in the number sentence below?

$6 \times n = 1$

Ⓐ $\frac{3}{6}$ Ⓒ $\frac{6}{6}$

Ⓑ $\frac{1}{6}$ Ⓓ 1

9. What is .045 expressed as a percent?

Ⓐ 0.045%   Ⓒ 4.50%

Ⓑ 0.45%   Ⓓ 45.0%

10. Use the number line below to solve the number sentence.

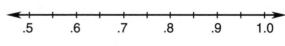

$.55 + .15 = \square$

Ⓐ .65   Ⓒ .75

Ⓑ .70   Ⓓ 1.0

GO ON ▷

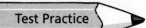
Math Tryout Test 1 (continued)

11.
$$\begin{array}{r} 2001 \\ 1963 \\ 33 \\ + 400 \end{array}$$

Ⓐ 4396
Ⓑ 4397
Ⓒ 4407
Ⓓ 4694
Ⓔ NG

12.
$$\begin{array}{r} 101 \\ \times 990 \end{array}$$

Ⓐ 99,990
Ⓑ 99,909
Ⓒ 90,990
Ⓓ 18,180
Ⓔ NG

13.
$$\frac{9}{10} - \frac{2}{5} =$$

Ⓐ $\frac{4}{5}$
Ⓑ $\frac{7}{10}$
Ⓒ $\frac{1}{2}$
Ⓓ $\frac{2}{5}$
Ⓔ NG

14.
$$2\frac{1}{5} \times 3\frac{1}{2} =$$

Ⓐ $1\frac{4}{5}$
Ⓑ $5\frac{1}{7}$
Ⓒ $6\frac{1}{10}$
Ⓓ $7\frac{7}{10}$
Ⓔ NG

15.
$$11.34 \div .81 =$$

Ⓐ 14.0
Ⓑ 1.40
Ⓒ .140
Ⓓ .014
Ⓔ NG

16.
$$35\% \text{ of } 120 =$$

Ⓐ 35
Ⓑ 42
Ⓒ 47
Ⓓ 57
Ⓔ NG

17. Dave read the following number of pages in his book each day for 5 days: 34, 21, 25, 41, 39. What was the average number of pages he read per day?

Ⓐ 22
Ⓓ 41
Ⓑ 31
Ⓔ NG
Ⓒ 32

18. What is the probability of spinning "Spin Again" on the first spin?

Ⓐ $\frac{1}{6}$
Ⓓ $\frac{2}{2}$
Ⓑ $\frac{1}{3}$
Ⓔ NG
Ⓒ $\frac{1}{2}$

19. The Buy-Low store has cassette tapes on sale at 6 for $9.99. At this rate, how much will 2 tapes cost?

Ⓐ $1.67
Ⓓ $4.99
Ⓑ $3.30
Ⓔ NG
Ⓒ $3.33

20. Eric's birds eat 5 pounds of bird food a week. He has asked his friend Karen to feed the birds while he is away for 10 days. How many pounds of bird food must he leave so that Karen will not run out?

Ⓐ 7 lb
Ⓓ 25 lb
Ⓑ 8 lb
Ⓔ NG
Ⓒ 10 lb

GO ON

21. Lee gets a 15% discount on clothes that she buys at the Clothes Horse, where she works. Last week she bought a $30 skirt and a $15 shirt. How much did she save on her total purchase?

    Ⓐ $2.25   Ⓒ $6.75   Ⓔ NG
    Ⓑ $3.50   Ⓓ $15.00

22. Kate makes $4.00 an hour helping at the local daycare center and $3.00 an hour babysitting. If she works 5 hours at the daycare center and babysits for 4 hours, how much will she earn?

    Ⓐ $15   Ⓒ $32   Ⓔ NG
    Ⓑ $20   Ⓓ $63

23. Greg had homework in math, science, and English. He spent 45 minutes on his science homework and 30 minutes on English. If he spent 2 hours on his homework in all, which number sentence should you use to find out how long he spent on math?

    Ⓐ $120 - (45 + 30) = \square$

    Ⓑ $(45 + 30) \div 2 = \square$

    Ⓒ $(45 + 30) - \square = 120$

    Ⓓ $2 + (45 - 30) = \square$

    Ⓔ NG

24. Kevin and his mother made an 8 gallon pot of soup for a soup kitchen. What other information do you need to know to find out how many bowls of soup this will make?

    Ⓐ how many people eat at the kitchen

    Ⓑ how many bowls of soup each person is allowed to have

    Ⓒ how often Kevin and his mother bring food to the kitchen

    Ⓓ how many other people have brought food to the kitchen

    Ⓔ how much soup each bowl holds

25. If $250 = x - 35$, $x =$

    Ⓐ 215   Ⓒ 275   Ⓔ NG
    Ⓑ 225   Ⓓ 285

26. If $x + 23 = 79$, $x =$

    Ⓐ 46   Ⓒ 92   Ⓔ NG
    Ⓑ 56   Ⓓ 102

27. If $12y = 168$, $y =$

    Ⓐ 13   Ⓒ 156   Ⓔ NG
    Ⓑ 14   Ⓓ 180

Use the graph to answer questions 28–30.

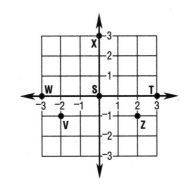

28. Which point is at (3,0)?

    Ⓐ T   Ⓓ X
    Ⓑ V   Ⓔ NG
    Ⓒ W

29. Where is point Z located?

    Ⓐ (−2,−1)   Ⓓ (2,−1)
    Ⓑ (2,1)   Ⓔ NG
    Ⓒ (−1,2)

30. Which point is located on the y-axis?

    Ⓐ V   Ⓓ X
    Ⓑ T   Ⓔ NG
    Ⓒ W

Math Tryout Test 1 (continued)

31. The figures below are congruent. Which side in figure 2 corresponds to side $\overline{AF}$ in figure 1?

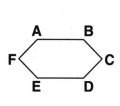
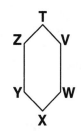

Fig. 1   Fig. 2

Ⓐ $\overline{TV}$ Ⓒ $\overline{YZ}$ Ⓔ NG

Ⓑ $\overline{WX}$ Ⓓ $\overline{VW}$

32. Which is a right triangle?

Ⓐ

Ⓑ

Ⓒ

Ⓓ

Ⓔ

33. Point P is the intersection of which two lines?

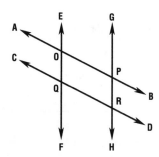

Ⓐ AB and EF   Ⓓ EF and CD

Ⓑ GH and CD   Ⓔ GH and AB

Ⓒ CD and AB

34. Which of these is an acute angle?

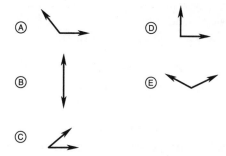

Ⓐ   Ⓓ

Ⓑ   Ⓔ

Ⓒ

35. What is the circumference of the circle below? ($\pi = 3.14$)

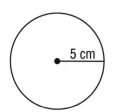

5 cm

Ⓐ 5 cm

Ⓑ 10 cm

Ⓒ 15.7 cm

Ⓓ 31.4 cm

Ⓔ NG

36. What is the volume of this box?

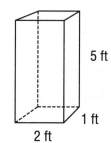

5 ft

1 ft

2 ft

Ⓐ 7 cu ft

Ⓑ 8 cu ft

Ⓒ 10 cu ft

Ⓓ 11 cu ft

Ⓔ NG

37. Which statement would most help to prove that $\overline{AC}$ is perpendicular to $\overline{BD}$?

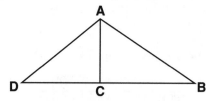

Ⓐ ∠ABD < 90°.

Ⓑ ∠BAC is acute.

Ⓒ ∠ABD < ∠ACB

Ⓓ ∠ABC is not congruent to ∠ABD.

Ⓔ ∠CAB + ∠CBA = 90°.

GO ON

38. The school band met to get ready for the town parade at 8:00. The band spent 30 minutes practicing music and 15 minutes lining up for the parade. The parade itself took $2\frac{1}{2}$ hours. Which clock shows what time the band got finished with the parade?

Ⓐ Ⓒ

Ⓑ Ⓓ

39. Marty wants to build a pen for his dog in the backyard. What unit of measurement should he use to find out how much fencing to buy?

Ⓐ inch Ⓒ foot

Ⓑ mile Ⓓ ounce

40. Hilary has two sacks of potatoes that weigh 4.9 pounds each and a sack of onions that weighs a little more than $2\frac{1}{2}$ pounds. About how much do the sacks weigh all together?

Ⓐ $10\frac{1}{2}$ lb Ⓒ 12 lb

Ⓑ 11 lb Ⓓ $12\frac{1}{2}$ lb

This graph shows the monthly rainfall in Millersville in 1985 and in 1990. Use it to answer questions 41–44.

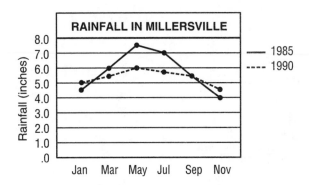

41. Which was the rainiest month in both years?

Ⓐ January Ⓒ May

Ⓑ March Ⓓ November

42. How many inches of rain fell in Millersville in July 1990?

Ⓐ 5.0 in Ⓒ 5.7 in

Ⓑ 5.3 in Ⓓ 7.0 in

43. In which month did the same amount of rain fall in both 1985 and 1990?

Ⓐ September Ⓒ March

Ⓑ January Ⓓ November

44. How much more rain fell in November 1990 than in November 1985?

Ⓐ .1 in Ⓒ 1 in

Ⓑ .6 in Ⓓ 1.6 in

Number Correct/Total = _____ /44

Whole Number Concepts

Recognizing, comparing, ordering, and factoring numerals

Directions: Choose the best answer for each question.

A What number is 10,000 more than 425,673,890?

- Ⓐ 426,673,890
- Ⓑ 425,773,890
- Ⓒ 435,673,890
- Ⓓ 425,683,890

B What is another name for three hundred forty thousand, one hundred forty?

- Ⓐ 340,104
- Ⓑ 340,140
- Ⓒ 340,000,140
- Ⓓ 340,000,104

Only 10,000 more

These questions are about **renaming**, **comparing**, and **ordering** numbers. In Example A, the question asks you to find the number that is 10,000 more than 425,673,890. To answer this question, first find the ten thousands place. This number has a 7 in the ten thousands place. If you add 10,000 to this number, there will be an 8 in the ten thousands place. The correct answer is choice Ⓓ, *425,683,890.*

Example B asks you to rename three hundred forty thousand, one hundred forty. To answer this question, you can write the numbers in a chart like this.

100,000's	10,000's	1000's	100's	10's	1's
3	4	0	1	4	0

Or, you can look at the answer choices and read each one as number words. Choice Ⓑ, *340,140,* is correct. Notice that this is the same number written in the chart.

Now look at some more test question examples.

C What is the greatest common factor of 45 and 72?

- Ⓐ 3
- Ⓒ 15
- Ⓑ 9
- Ⓓ 24

D What is the least common multiple of 15 and 20?

- Ⓐ 30
- Ⓒ 60
- Ⓑ 40
- Ⓓ 120

These questions are about finding **factors** and **multiples**. Example C asks you to find the greatest common factor of two numbers. To find the greatest common factor, first find all of the factors of each number. List the factors common to both and find the common factor with the greatest value. In Example C, only 3 and 9 are factors common to both 45 and 72. Answer Ⓑ, *9*, is the greatest common factor.

Example D asks you to find the least common multiple of two numbers. To find multiples, multiply each number times the factors in the multiplication table (1×15, 2×15, 3×15, etc.). List the multiples of each number until you find the least multiple common to both numbers. The correct answer is Ⓒ, *60* (4×15 and 3×20).

Now look at these examples.

E What is -5×3?

 Ⓐ -2

 Ⓑ -15

 Ⓒ 15

 Ⓓ 8

F Find *y* in this number sentence.

$$43 + (20 + 11) = (43 + 20) + y$$

 Ⓐ 63   Ⓒ 11

 Ⓑ 33   Ⓓ 9

These questions are about **properties of numbers** and **operations**. Example E involves multiplication with an **integer**, or negative number. To find the answer, multiply 5×3 and add a negative sign to the answer. When you multiply a negative times a positive, the answer is always negative. The correct answer is Ⓑ, *−15*.

In Example F, you can find *y* if you know the **properties of addition**. It does not matter where the parentheses are placed in this number sentence. The sum remains the same no matter which numbers are in parentheses. The same numbers would appear on both sides of the number sentence ($43 + 20 + 11 = 43 + 20 + 11$). So the correct response is Ⓒ, *11*.

Test-Taking Tips

1 Look for key words in each question. (In Example A, the key words are *more than*. In Example D, the key word is *least*.)

2 Try out each answer choice until you find the one that is correct.

Go for it

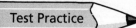

Test Practice 1: Whole Number Concepts   Time: **20** minutes

Directions: Choose the best answer for each question.

1. What is the numeral for seventy-eight million, thirty thousand one hundred?

   Ⓐ 78,300,100

   Ⓑ 780,030,100

   Ⓒ 78,030,100

   Ⓓ 78,310,000

2. Which number is closest to the value of 10,000?

   Ⓐ 10,120   Ⓒ 9899

   Ⓑ 10,098   Ⓓ 9955

3. Which number is less than 321,211?

   Ⓐ 321,221   Ⓒ 331,201

   Ⓑ 321,201   Ⓓ 322,122

4. Which is another name for 47?

   Ⓐ $(8 \times 5) + 7$

   Ⓑ $(4 + 10) + 7$

   Ⓒ $(5 \times 10) - 4$

   Ⓓ $(49 \div 7) + 4$

5. What is the value of the 3 in 43,567,121?

   Ⓐ 30,000,000

   Ⓑ 300,000

   Ⓒ 3,000,000

   Ⓓ 30,000

6. What is 177,569 rounded to the nearest hundred?

   Ⓐ 178,000

   Ⓑ 177,600

   Ⓒ 200,000

   Ⓓ 177,500

7. Which is another name for 4750?

   Ⓐ $(47 \times 10) + (5 \times 10)$

   Ⓑ $(4 \times 100) + (7 \times 10) + (5 \times 1)$

   Ⓒ $(4 \times 10,000) + (75 \times 10)$

   Ⓓ $(4 \times 1000) + (7 \times 100) + (5 \times 10)$

8. What number is expressed by

   $$(6 \times 10^4) + (4 \times 10^3) + (8 \times 10^2)$$?

   Ⓐ 64,800   Ⓒ 640,800

   Ⓑ 6,408,000   Ⓓ 6480

9. $$7^2 - 9 = \square$$

   Ⓐ 5   Ⓒ 30

   Ⓑ 15   Ⓓ 40

10. Which is another name for 56,890,100?

    Ⓐ five hundred sixty million, eighty-nine thousand one

    Ⓑ fifty-six thousand, eight hundred ninety-one

    Ⓒ fifty-six million, eight hundred ninety thousand, one hundred

    Ⓓ fifty-six million, eighty-nine thousand, one hundred

11. Which is a prime number?

    Ⓐ 232   Ⓒ 431

    Ⓑ 147   Ⓓ 315

12. Which is a composite number?

    Ⓐ 11   Ⓒ 31

    Ⓑ 23   Ⓓ 63

GO ON ➡

13. $815 \div 20$ is closest to —

Ⓐ 40   Ⓒ 42
Ⓑ 41   Ⓓ 43

14. Which number is a factor of 102?

Ⓐ 8   Ⓒ 13
Ⓑ 10   Ⓓ 17

15. What are the prime factors of 64?

Ⓐ 2, 3   Ⓒ 1, 2
Ⓑ 1, 4   Ⓓ 2, 8

16. What is the greatest common factor of 21 and 63?

Ⓐ 3   Ⓒ 9
Ⓑ 7   Ⓓ 21

17. Which number is a multiple of 12?

Ⓐ 3   Ⓒ 32
Ⓑ 4   Ⓓ 48

18. What is the least common multiple of 30 and 42?

Ⓐ 84   Ⓒ 210
Ⓑ 96   Ⓓ 1260

19. What is the square root of 36?

Ⓐ 6   Ⓒ 72
Ⓑ 18   Ⓓ 1296

20. Use the number line to complete the operation below.

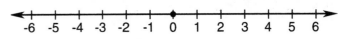

$-5 + 2 + -3 = \square$

Ⓐ 6   Ⓒ 4
Ⓑ −6   Ⓓ −1

21. $7 \times -8 = \square$

Ⓐ −1   Ⓒ −56
Ⓑ −15   Ⓓ 56

22. Find n in this number sentence.

$14 \times (5 + n) = (14 \times 5) + (14 \times 2)$

Ⓐ 2   Ⓒ 28
Ⓑ 21   Ⓓ 70

23. Solve for n.

$12 \times 4 = n \times 12$

Ⓐ 3   Ⓒ 8
Ⓑ 4   Ⓓ 16

24. Find n in this number sentence.

$n + (42 + 21) = (11 + 42) + 21$

Ⓐ 63   Ⓒ 32
Ⓑ 53   Ⓓ 11

STOP

Number Correct/Total = _____ /24

Fractions, Decimals, and Percents

Comparing and renaming fractions, decimals, and percents

I'm 10% taller

Directions: Choose the best answer for each question.

A Which fraction has the same value as $8\frac{2}{3}$?

    Ⓐ $\frac{10}{3}$ Ⓒ $\frac{24}{3}$

    Ⓑ $\frac{16}{3}$ Ⓓ $\frac{26}{3}$

B What is 33% expressed as a decimal?

    Ⓐ .033   Ⓒ 3.3

    Ⓑ .33   Ⓓ 33.0

In Example A, you must rename the **mixed number** $8\frac{2}{3}$ as an **improper fraction** with the denominator 3. To do this, follow the steps below.

1) Multiply the denominator of the fraction $\frac{2}{3}$ by the whole number 8: $3 \times 8 = 24$.

2) Add the result (24) to the numerator of the fraction $\frac{2}{3}$: $24 + 2 = 26$.

So, $8\frac{2}{3}$ is the same as $\frac{26}{3}$. You can check your answer by dividing to change the improper fraction $\frac{26}{3}$ back into a mixed number. $26 \div 3 = 8$ R2, or $8\frac{2}{3}$. The correct answer is Ⓓ.

Example B asks you to convert a percent into a decimal. **Percent** means *hundredths*. Look at the chart to understand how percents relate to fractions and decimals.

1%	10%	100%
$\frac{1}{100} = .01$	$\frac{10}{100} = .10$	$\frac{100}{100} = 1.00$

Since 33% means the same as "thirty-three hundredths," or $\frac{33}{100}$, it equals .33. Choice Ⓑ is correct.

Test-Taking Tips

1 Look for key words and numbers in each question. (In Example A, the key words are *same value*. The key number is $8\frac{2}{3}$. In Example B, the key word is *decimal*. The key number is *33%*.)

2 When comparing fractions, rename unlike fractions and mixed numbers to be like fractions (with the same denominator). Example: $\frac{2}{3} > \frac{3}{5}$ can be renamed as $\frac{10}{15} > \frac{9}{15}$.

3 Remember that *percent* means *hundredths* ($33\% = \frac{33}{100} = .33$).

Go for it

Test Practice 2:
Fractions, Decimals, and Percents

Time: **20** minutes

Directions: Choose the best answer for each question.

1. What fraction is another name for $\frac{5}{6}$?

   Ⓐ $\frac{30}{36}$ Ⓒ $\frac{15}{16}$

   Ⓑ $\frac{20}{25}$ Ⓓ $\frac{12}{15}$

2. What is the simplest name for $\frac{16}{48}$?

   Ⓐ $\frac{2}{6}$ Ⓒ $\frac{4}{12}$

   Ⓑ $\frac{1}{3}$ Ⓓ $\frac{1}{4}$

3. What fraction has the same value as $\frac{55}{100}$?

   Ⓐ $\frac{5}{10}$ Ⓒ $\frac{11}{20}$

   Ⓑ $\frac{5}{11}$ Ⓓ $\frac{11}{25}$

4. Which fraction goes in the box?

   $$\frac{1}{4} = \square$$

   Ⓐ $\frac{12}{36}$ Ⓒ $\frac{12}{24}$

   Ⓑ $\frac{45}{60}$ Ⓓ $\frac{15}{60}$

5. Which fraction best completes this number sentence?

   $$4\frac{7}{8} = \square$$

   Ⓐ $\frac{39}{8}$ Ⓒ $\frac{31}{8}$

   Ⓑ $\frac{32}{8}$ Ⓓ $\frac{11}{8}$

6. Which group of fractions is in order from least to greatest?

   Ⓐ $\frac{9}{81}, \frac{8}{40}, \frac{6}{36}, \frac{4}{32}$

   Ⓑ $\frac{9}{81}, \frac{4}{32}, \frac{6}{36}, \frac{8}{40}$

   Ⓒ $\frac{8}{40}, \frac{6}{36}, \frac{9}{81}, \frac{4}{32}$

   Ⓓ $\frac{4}{32}, \frac{6}{36}, \frac{8}{40}, \frac{9}{81}$

7. Which fraction best completes the number sentence?

   $$\frac{24}{9} > \square$$

   Ⓐ $2\frac{4}{9}$ Ⓒ $2\frac{8}{9}$

   Ⓑ $2\frac{2}{3}$ Ⓓ $2\frac{14}{18}$

8. Which number fits in the box?

   $$\frac{1}{6} \times \square = 1$$

   Ⓐ $\frac{1}{6}$ Ⓒ 1

   Ⓑ $\frac{6}{6}$ Ⓓ 6

9. Which number completes the number sentence?

   $$\frac{1}{20} \times 20 = \square$$

   Ⓐ $\frac{1}{10}$ Ⓒ 20

   Ⓑ $\frac{1}{40}$ Ⓓ 1

10. Which fraction is another name for .02?

   Ⓐ $\frac{2}{20}$ Ⓒ $\frac{2}{100}$

   Ⓑ $\frac{2}{10}$ Ⓓ $\frac{20}{100}$

GO ON ➤

11. What is $\frac{6}{100}$ expressed as a percent?

   Ⓐ .6%   Ⓒ 60%

   Ⓑ 6.0%   Ⓓ 600%

12. Which number sentence is true?

   Ⓐ 78% = .78

   Ⓑ 78% = 7.8

   Ⓒ 78% = .078

   Ⓓ 78% = 78.0

13. What number is 4 tenths more than 35.505?

   Ⓐ 39.505   Ⓒ 35.545

   Ⓑ 35.905   Ⓓ 35.509

14. Which decimal has the least value?

   Ⓐ .224   Ⓒ .241

   Ⓑ .214   Ⓓ .242

15. What is the value of the 7 in 24.735?

   Ⓐ $\frac{7}{10}$ Ⓒ $\frac{7}{1000}$

   Ⓑ $\frac{7}{100}$ Ⓓ $\frac{7}{1}$

16. In which number does the 4 have a value of $\frac{4}{100}$?

   Ⓐ 45.978   Ⓒ 31.489

   Ⓑ 94.365   Ⓓ 56.741

17. What is .8945 rounded to the nearest hundredth?

   Ⓐ .90   Ⓒ .895

   Ⓑ .89   Ⓓ .894

18. What is 7.917 rounded to the nearest tenth?

   Ⓐ 8.0   Ⓒ 7.91

   Ⓑ 7.92   Ⓓ 7. 9

Use the number line below to answer questions 19–22.

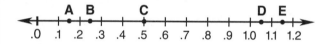

19. What decimal is $\frac{2}{10}$ more than .7?

   Ⓐ .6   Ⓒ .9

   Ⓑ .8   Ⓓ 1.1

20. Which point is located at 1.15?

   Ⓐ A   Ⓒ D

   Ⓑ C   Ⓓ E

21. Where is point C located?

   Ⓐ .45   Ⓒ .55

   Ⓑ .50   Ⓓ 1.5

22. What is .1 less than 1.2?

   Ⓐ 1.1   Ⓒ .20

   Ⓑ 1.0   Ⓓ .11

STOP

Number Correct/Total = _____ /22

Computing with Whole Numbers

Adding, subtracting, multiplying, and dividing whole numbers

Directions: Find the best answer for each question. If the correct answer is not given, mark NG.

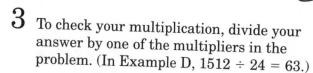

A

3668
− 697

Ⓐ 2961
Ⓑ 2971
Ⓒ 3071
Ⓓ 3081
Ⓔ NG

B

987 ÷ 21 =

Ⓐ 57
Ⓑ 47 R2
Ⓒ 47
Ⓓ 46 R1
Ⓔ NG

Example A is a subtraction problem. Subtract the numbers in each column, and don't forget to borrow from the next column as needed. 3668 − 697 = 2971. Choice Ⓑ is correct. The other choices all have errors in subtracting one or more of the columns. To solve Example B, you have to divide. 987 ÷ 21 = 47. Since 987 can be divided evenly by 21, there is no remainder. Choice Ⓒ, *47*, is correct. Now try these problems.

C

7201
+ 3909

Ⓐ 10,100
Ⓑ 11,100
Ⓒ 11,200
Ⓓ 11,210
Ⓔ NG

D

63
× 24

Ⓐ 1402
Ⓑ 1502
Ⓒ 1512
Ⓓ 3672
Ⓔ NG

To solve Example C, add the numbers. 7201 + 3909 = 11,110. But, 11,110 is not given as an answer choice, so the correct choice is Ⓔ, NG. To solve Example D, multiply: 63 × 24 = 1512. Choice Ⓒ is correct.

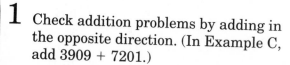

Test-Taking Tips

1 Check addition problems by adding in the opposite direction. (In Example C, add 3909 + 7201.)

2 Check your subtraction by adding. (In Example A, add your answer to the smaller number or *subtrahend*: 2971 + 697 = 3668.)

3 To check your multiplication, divide your answer by one of the multipliers in the problem. (In Example D, 1512 ÷ 24 = 63.)

4 To check your division, multiply the answer by the divisor. (In Example B, 47 × 21 = 987.)

Go for it

Test Practice 3: Computing with Whole Numbers Time: 20 minutes

Directions: Choose the best answer for each question.

1.
8356
+ 2139

Ⓐ 9485
Ⓑ 10,485
Ⓒ 10,495
Ⓓ 10,595
Ⓔ NG

7.
8236
− 1457

Ⓐ 7789
Ⓑ 6889
Ⓒ 6789
Ⓓ 6779
Ⓔ NG

2.
563
952
+ 87

Ⓐ 1482
Ⓑ 1502
Ⓒ 1582
Ⓓ 1602
Ⓔ NG

8.
22019
− 3996

Ⓐ 25,023
Ⓑ 19,015
Ⓒ 18,123
Ⓓ 18,023
Ⓔ NG

3.
3238
875
+ 7475

Ⓐ 11,588
Ⓑ 11,578
Ⓒ 11,488
Ⓓ 11,478
Ⓔ NG

9.
1661
− 669

Ⓐ 1012
Ⓑ 1002
Ⓒ 992
Ⓓ 982
Ⓔ NG

4.
1492
1066
481
+ 44

Ⓐ 2983
Ⓑ 3073
Ⓒ 3083
Ⓓ 3183
Ⓔ NG

10.
561
− 83

Ⓐ 468
Ⓑ 478
Ⓒ 488
Ⓓ 568
Ⓔ NG

5.
6979
7205
+ 11

Ⓐ 13,195
Ⓑ 14,084
Ⓒ 14,185
Ⓓ 14,205
Ⓔ NG

11.
1323
− 989

Ⓐ 334
Ⓑ 343
Ⓒ 433
Ⓓ 434
Ⓔ NG

6.
512
714
+ 938

Ⓐ 2254
Ⓑ 2164
Ⓒ 2154
Ⓓ 2064
Ⓔ NG

12.
4862
− 2968

Ⓐ 1804
Ⓑ 1884
Ⓒ 1904
Ⓓ 1994
Ⓔ NG

GO ON

13.

$6 \times 832 =$

Ⓐ 4832
Ⓑ 4882
Ⓒ 4892
Ⓓ 4992
Ⓔ NG

14.

$\begin{array}{r} 69 \\ \times\ 36 \\ \hline \end{array}$

Ⓐ 2474
Ⓑ 2484
Ⓒ 2774
Ⓓ 2784
Ⓔ NG

15.

$\begin{array}{r} 186 \\ \times\ 97 \\ \hline \end{array}$

Ⓐ 19,057
Ⓑ 18,042
Ⓒ 2857
Ⓓ 1842
Ⓔ NG

16.

$\begin{array}{r} 361 \\ \times\ 32 \\ \hline \end{array}$

Ⓐ 9824
Ⓑ 9852
Ⓒ 11,552
Ⓓ 12,624
Ⓔ NG

17.

$\begin{array}{r} 806 \\ \times\ 679 \\ \hline \end{array}$

Ⓐ 554,074
Ⓑ 547,204
Ⓒ 547,156
Ⓓ 544,256
Ⓔ NG

18.

$\begin{array}{r} 111 \\ \times\ 77 \\ \hline \end{array}$

Ⓐ 7447
Ⓑ 7777
Ⓒ 8547
Ⓓ 8777
Ⓔ NG

19.

$82 \overline{)4660}$

Ⓐ $58\frac{17}{21}$
Ⓑ $56\frac{17}{21}$
Ⓒ $56\frac{34}{41}$
Ⓓ 56
Ⓔ NG

20.

$2392 \div 22 =$

Ⓐ $108\frac{8}{22}$
Ⓑ $108\frac{6}{11}$
Ⓒ $106\frac{8}{11}$
Ⓓ $106\frac{6}{11}$
Ⓔ NG

21.

$341 \overline{)9889}$

Ⓐ 28 R 153
Ⓑ 28 R 53
Ⓒ 29 R 53
Ⓓ 29
Ⓔ NG

22.

$1562 \div 8 =$

Ⓐ $192\frac{1}{4}$
Ⓑ $192\frac{5}{8}$
Ⓒ $195\frac{2}{8}$
Ⓓ $195\frac{3}{4}$
Ⓔ NG

23.

$12 \overline{)878}$

Ⓐ $72\frac{2}{12}$
Ⓑ $72\frac{1}{3}$
Ⓒ $73\frac{1}{6}$
Ⓓ $72\frac{1}{3}$
Ⓔ NG

24.

$66 \overline{)7020}$

Ⓐ $106\frac{4}{11}$
Ⓑ $108\frac{6}{11}$
Ⓒ $116\frac{4}{11}$
Ⓓ $116\frac{6}{11}$
Ⓔ NG

Number Correct/Total = _____ /24

115

Computing with Fractions, Decimals, and Percents

Adding, subtracting, multiplying, and dividing fractions, mixed numbers, and decimals; finding percents

Directions: Choose the best answer for each question.

A

$$13\frac{3}{5}$$
$$-\ 7\frac{2}{3}$$

Ⓐ $6\frac{1}{2}$

Ⓑ $6\frac{1}{5}$

Ⓒ $6\frac{1}{15}$

Ⓓ $5\frac{14}{15}$

Ⓔ NG

B

4% of $\$25.00 =$

Ⓐ $\$.62$

Ⓑ $\$1.00$

Ⓒ $\$6.25$

Ⓓ $\$10.00$

Ⓔ NG

To subtract the mixed numbers in Example A, you must first rename the fractional parts to have the same denominator. The **lowest common denominator** for 5 and 3 is 15.

$$13\frac{3}{5} \quad = \quad 13\frac{9}{15}$$
$$-\ 7\frac{2}{3} \qquad\quad -\ 7\frac{10}{15}$$

Since $\frac{10}{15}$ is greater than $\frac{9}{15}$, you must borrow a 1 ($\frac{15}{15}$) from the whole number 13 and add it to the fraction $\frac{9}{15}$.

When you add the borrowed 1, then $13\frac{9}{15}$ becomes $12\frac{24}{15}$. Notice how you must change the 1 to a fraction, $\frac{15}{15}$, before you can add it to $\frac{9}{15}$. Now you can solve the problem: $12\frac{24}{15} - 7\frac{10}{15} = 5\frac{14}{15}$. Choice Ⓓ is correct.

In Example B, you must find 4 percent of $\$25.00$. To do this, first write a number sentence that shows what you want to find and how to find it. Replace the word "of" with a multiplication sign. $4\% \times \$25.00 = ?$ Then convert the percent into a decimal: $4\% = \frac{4}{100} = .04$. Now solve the number sentence: $.04 \times \$25.00 = \$1.00$. Choice Ⓑ is correct.

4% SALE

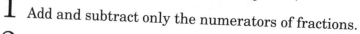

Test-Taking Tips

1 Add and subtract only the numerators of fractions.

2 Rename fractions with different denominators as like fractions. (In Example A, you rename $13\frac{3}{5}$ as $13\frac{9}{15}$ and $7\frac{2}{3}$ as $7\frac{10}{15}$.)

3 When working with percents, first write a number sentence to help you solve the problem. Then convert the percent to a decimal and solve the number sentence. (In Example B, 4% of $\$25.00 = .04 \times \$25.00 = \$1.00$.)

Go for it

Test Practice 4: Computing with Fractions, Decimals, and Percents

Time: **20** minutes

Directions: Choose the best answer for each question.

1.

$1.049 + .937 =$

- (A) 2.077
- (B) 1.976
- (C) 1.986
- (D) 2.086
- (E) NG

2.

$32.51 + 37.09 + 6.8 =$

- (A) 76.28
- (B) 76.38
- (C) 76.47
- (D) 75.40
- (E) NG

3.

$11.6 - 3.33 =$

- (A) 8.27
- (B) 8.33
- (C) 8.37
- (D) 8.93
- (E) NG

4.

$156.2 - 18.8 =$

- (A) 138.6
- (B) 138.4
- (C) 137.4
- (D) 136.6
- (E) NG

5.

$32.619 \times 60 =$

- (A) 1.95714
- (B) 19.5714
- (C) 195.714
- (D) 1957.14
- (E) NG

6.

$4.00 \times 12.846 =$

- (A) .51384
- (B) 5.1384
- (C) 51.384
- (D) 513.84
- (E) NG

7.

$3.69 \times .003 =$

- (A) .001107
- (B) .011070
- (C) .110700
- (D) 1.10700
- (E) NG

8.

$4.9 \div 7.0 =$

- (A) 70.0
- (B) 7.00
- (C) 0.70
- (D) 0.07
- (E) NG

9.

$25.6 \div 0.16 =$

- (A) 0.16
- (B) 1.60
- (C) 16.0
- (D) 1600
- (E) NG

10.

$.32 \div .8 =$

- (A) 0.04
- (B) 0.40
- (C) 4.0
- (D) 40.0
- (E) NG

11.

$\frac{3}{7} + \frac{6}{7} =$

- (A) $1\frac{3}{7}$
- (B) $1\frac{2}{7}$
- (C) $\frac{9}{14}$
- (D) $\frac{18}{49}$
- (E) NG

12.

$3\frac{2}{3} + 5\frac{1}{4} =$

- (A) $8\frac{3}{12}$
- (B) $8\frac{3}{7}$
- (C) $8\frac{5}{6}$
- (D) $8\frac{11}{12}$
- (E) NG

GO ON

117

13.
$$7\frac{8}{11}$$
$$+\ 4\frac{5}{11}$$

Ⓐ $3\frac{13}{11}$
Ⓑ $12\frac{13}{11}$
Ⓒ $12\frac{2}{22}$
Ⓓ $11\frac{13}{22}$
Ⓔ NG

14.
$$\frac{9}{24} - \frac{1}{8} =$$

Ⓐ $\frac{3}{4}$
Ⓑ $\frac{1}{2}$
Ⓒ $\frac{1}{3}$
Ⓓ $\frac{1}{4}$
Ⓔ NG

15.
$$4\frac{1}{6}$$
$$-\ 1\frac{2}{3}$$

Ⓐ $2\frac{1}{2}$
Ⓑ $2\frac{2}{3}$
Ⓒ $3\frac{1}{3}$
Ⓓ $3\frac{1}{2}$
Ⓔ NG

16.
$$2\frac{1}{3} - \frac{5}{6} =$$

Ⓐ $1\frac{1}{6}$
Ⓑ $1\frac{1}{3}$
Ⓒ $1\frac{1}{2}$
Ⓓ $1\frac{5}{6}$
Ⓔ NG

17.
$$\frac{5}{9} \times \frac{9}{10} =$$

Ⓐ $\frac{4}{9}$
Ⓑ $\frac{1}{3}$
Ⓒ $\frac{5}{9}$
Ⓓ $\frac{50}{81}$
Ⓔ NG

18.
$$3\frac{1}{8} \times 1\frac{1}{3} =$$

Ⓐ $4\frac{1}{12}$
Ⓑ $4\frac{1}{8}$
Ⓒ $4\frac{1}{6}$
Ⓓ $4\frac{1}{4}$
Ⓔ NG

19.
$$\frac{11}{16} \div \frac{3}{8} =$$

Ⓐ $\frac{33}{16}$
Ⓑ $\frac{11}{6}$
Ⓒ $\frac{11}{16}$
Ⓓ $\frac{33}{128}$
Ⓔ NG

20.
$$6\frac{1}{4} \div 25 =$$

Ⓐ $\frac{6}{100}$
Ⓑ $\frac{4}{25}$
Ⓒ $\frac{1}{4}$
Ⓓ $\frac{25}{6}$
Ⓔ NG

21.
36% of $12.00 =

Ⓐ $4.32
Ⓑ $43.20
Ⓒ $432.00
Ⓓ $4320.00
Ⓔ NG

22.
4 is what % of 200?

Ⓐ 2
Ⓑ 5
Ⓒ 20
Ⓓ 25
Ⓔ NG

23.
175% of 16 =

Ⓐ 12
Ⓑ 20
Ⓒ 32
Ⓓ 64
Ⓔ NG

24.
21 is what % of 6?

Ⓐ 3.5
Ⓑ 35
Ⓒ 350
Ⓓ 3500
Ⓔ NG

STOP

Number Correct/Total = _____ /24

Statistics and Probability

Finding average, mean, median, and probability

Directions: Choose the best answer for each question.

A The low temperatures for three days in San Francisco were 52°, 59°, and 57°. What was the average low temperature over those three days?

Ⓐ 52°   Ⓓ 59°

Ⓑ 55°   Ⓔ NG

Ⓒ 56°

B A six-sided cube has two red sides, three blue sides, and one green side. What is the probability of landing with the red side up if you throw the cube once?

Ⓐ $\frac{4}{6}$ Ⓓ $\frac{2}{5}$

Ⓑ $\frac{1}{2}$ Ⓔ NG

Ⓒ $\frac{1}{3}$

Example A asks you to find the **average** of three numbers. To find an average, first add the numbers you are given: $52 + 59 + 57 = 168$. Then divide that result by the number of figures you added. In this example, you added three numbers, so $168 \div 3 = 56$. The average low temperature in San Francisco over the three days was 56°. Choice Ⓒ is correct.

Other test questions may ask you to find the mean or median of a set of numbers. In these questions, the **mean** is the same as the **average**. The **median** is the middle number in a set containing an odd number of items. For example, the median temperature in Example A is 57° because that is the middle number in the set: 54°, 57°, 59°. In a set with an even number of items, the median is halfway between the two middle numbers. For example, in the set 2,4,6,8,10,12, the median is 7 (halfway between 6 and 8).

Example B deals with probability. **Probability** defines the chances of some certain event occurring. If you flip a coin, there are two possible outcomes: heads or tails. The chance, or probability, of the coin coming up heads is 1 out of 2, or $\frac{1}{2}$.

Probability is usually expressed as a fraction:

P = number of possible ways/total number of ways

To find the probability of getting a red side in Example B, use the formula above: P = number of possible ways/ total number of ways = $\frac{2}{6} = \frac{1}{3}$. Choice Ⓒ is correct.

Test-Taking Tips

1 Look for key words to decide how to find the answer. (In Example A, the key word is *average*. In Example B, the key words are *probability* and *red*.)

2 Write down any information given to you in each problem. Draw pictures or make charts and tables if they will help you solve the problem.

Go for it

Test Practice 5: Statistics and Probability

Time: **10** minutes

Directions: Choose the best answer for each problem.

1. Rick had test scores of 81, 88, 93, and 90. What was his average score?

   Ⓐ 81   Ⓓ 88
   Ⓑ 84   Ⓔ NG
   Ⓒ 86

2. A clothing store made sales of $1500, $1200, $1350, $1250, and $1700 over 5 days. What was the median amount they earned?

   Ⓐ $1350   Ⓓ $1500
   Ⓑ $1400   Ⓔ NG
   Ⓒ $1450

3. The high temperatures in Tucson, Arizona, during the first week in July were 99°, 98°, 104°, 108°, 111°, 112°, and 103°. What was the median high temperature in Tucson that week?

   Ⓐ 100°   Ⓓ 108°
   Ⓑ 105°   Ⓔ NG
   Ⓒ 107°

4. Jolene read 34 pages of her book the day she started it. On the following days she read 42, 44, 29, and 31 pages. What was the average number of pages Jolene read each day?

   Ⓐ 36 pages   Ⓓ 44 pages
   Ⓑ 37 pages   Ⓔ NG
   Ⓒ 40 pages

Use the spinner to answer questions 5–6.

5. What is the probability of spinning a 2 on the first spin?

   Ⓐ $\frac{1}{2}$ Ⓓ $\frac{1}{6}$
   Ⓑ $\frac{2}{3}$ Ⓔ NG
   Ⓒ $\frac{1}{3}$

6. What is the probability of spinning a number from 1 to 5 on the first spin?

   Ⓐ $\frac{1}{3}$ Ⓓ $\frac{1}{2}$
   Ⓑ $\frac{2}{5}$ Ⓔ NG
   Ⓒ $\frac{3}{4}$

7. Grant's sister Lisa thought of a number from 11 to 20. What is the probability that Grant will guess the number correctly on the first try?

   Ⓐ $\frac{10}{20}$ Ⓓ $\frac{1}{5}$
   Ⓑ $\frac{1}{2}$ Ⓔ NG
   Ⓒ $\frac{1}{4}$

8. In a bin of surprise gifts, there are 25 pens, 15 super balls, and 5 gold pins. What is the probability that someone will get a gold pin with one pick?

   Ⓐ $\frac{1}{9}$ Ⓓ $\frac{40}{45}$
   Ⓑ $\frac{1}{8}$ Ⓔ NG
   Ⓒ $\frac{5}{50}$

STOP

Number Correct/Total = _____ /8

Problem Solving

Solving word problems

Directions: Choose the best answer for each question.

A Libby can swim a lap freestyle in 45 seconds. With the backstroke, she can swim a lap in 1 minute. Which number sentence should you use to find how long it will take her to swim 4 laps of each stroke?

Ⓐ $(45 \div 4) + (1 \div 4) = \square$

Ⓑ $(1 + 45) \times 4 = \square$

Ⓒ $(60 + 45) = 4 \times \square$

Ⓓ $4(45 + 60) = \square$

Ⓔ NG

B Doug made 5 phone calls last night. What else do you need to know to figure out how long Doug was on the phone?

Ⓐ what time he finished the last call

Ⓑ whom he called

Ⓒ what he talked about

Ⓓ what time he got on the phone

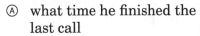
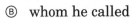

Ⓔ how many minutes each call took

Example A asks you to find the number sentence that will help you solve the problem. Look at the chart below.

Number of freestyle laps × time per lap + Number of backstroke laps × time per lap = total

4 × 45 seconds + 4 × 60 seconds = total

Notice that you must convert 1 minute to 60 seconds so that you will have like units. Now, you can write a number sentence like this: $(4 \times 45) + (4 \times 60) = \square$. By the **distributive property**, you can rewrite the number sentence like this: $4(45 + 60) = \square$. Choice Ⓓ is the correct number sentence to use.

Example B asks you to identify information needed to solve a problem. To find out how long Doug was on the phone all together, you would need to know how long each of his five calls took. It does not matter when he began, choice Ⓓ, when he finished, Ⓐ, whom he called, Ⓑ, or what he talked about, Ⓒ. Choice Ⓔ, how many minutes each call took, is all you would need to know to solve this problem.

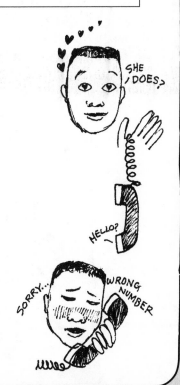

Now look at some more example test questions on page 122.

C There were 35 problems on the math test. Sue answered 28 of the questions correctly. What percent of the questions did Sue get right?

 Ⓐ 20%   Ⓓ 98%

 Ⓑ 75%   Ⓔ NG

 Ⓒ 80%

D The temperature in Blue Falls on Monday morning was 52°. By noon the temperature had risen 15°. The low temperature Monday night was 21° below the temperature at noon. What was the difference between the low temperature Monday night and the temperature that morning?

 Ⓐ 46°   Ⓓ 6°

 Ⓑ 36°   Ⓔ NG

 Ⓒ 16°

Example C asks you to find percent. You can solve this problem by following these four steps.

1) Write a number sentence that expresses the question. $28 = n \times 35$ (n stands for ?%)

2) Divide both sides by 35 to get n by itself. $28 \div 35 = n \times 35 \div 35$

3) Divide 28 by 35. $28 \div 35 = .80$

4) Express .80 as a percent. $.80 = \frac{80}{100} = 80\%$

Since $n = 80\%$, choice Ⓒ is the correct answer.

After you have practiced solving problems in this way, you can take the shortcut. You can write "28 equals what percent of 35?" as $\frac{28}{35} = n\%$, then solve it by dividing $\frac{28}{35}$.

Example D is a word problem with three steps. First, find the temperature at noon. It was 52° in the morning, and it rose 15°, so: $52° + 15° = 67°$. Then find the temperature at night. It dropped 21°, so: $67° - 21° = 46°$. The question asks for the difference between the low temperature Monday night and the temperature Monday morning, so you should subtract: $52° - 46° = 6°$. Choice Ⓓ is correct. The low temperature Monday night was 6° colder than the temperature Monday morning.

Test-Taking Tips

1 Look for key words and information as you read each problem. (In Example A, the key words are *how long.* Key information includes *45 seconds, 1 minute,* and *4 laps of each stroke.*)

2 Write down each piece of information given in the problem, and write down or circle what each problem asks you to find. When you figure out your answer, go back and make sure it answers the question you wrote down or circled.

Go for it

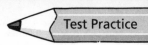

Test Practice 6: Problem Solving

Time: **15** minutes

Directions: Choose the best answer for each question.

1. Carlos scored 76, 89, and 92 on 3 math tests this term. What number sentence should you use to figure out Carlos's test average for the term?

   Ⓐ $3 \times (76 + 89 + 92) = \square$
   Ⓑ $(76 + 89 + 92) \div 3 = \square$
   Ⓒ $3 + (76 + 89 + 92) = \square$
   Ⓓ $(76 \times 89 \times 92) \div 3 = \square$
   Ⓔ NG

2. Andrea receives a 10% discount at Kidswear. Which number sentence should you use to find how much Andrea would pay for a shirt marked $22?

   Ⓐ $\$22 - (\$22 \times .10) = \square$
   Ⓑ $\$22 - 10 = \square$
   Ⓒ $(\$22 \times 10) - \$22 = \square$
   Ⓓ $\$22 \times .10 = \square$
   Ⓔ NG

3. Nicole's dog Bo eats 15 pounds of dry dog food a month. Her other dog Lad eats 20 pounds a month. How much dog food does it take to feed both dogs for 3 months?

   Ⓐ 35 lb   Ⓓ 105 lb
   Ⓑ 45 lb   Ⓔ NG
   Ⓒ 60 lb

4. A book of 10 stamps costs $2.50. If Hank buys 3 books of stamps, how much change should he receive from a $20 bill?

   Ⓐ $7.50   Ⓓ $17.50
   Ⓑ $10.00   Ⓔ NG
   Ⓒ $11.50

5. The 5-Mile Fun Run started at 8:00. Nancy ran each mile in 11 minutes. What time did Nancy finish the run?

   Ⓐ 8:16   Ⓓ 9:15
   Ⓑ 8:55   Ⓔ NG
   Ⓒ 9:05

6. Kip is now 5 feet tall. He has grown 4 inches in the last year. How tall was Kip a year ago?

   Ⓐ 5' 4"   Ⓓ 4' 6"
   Ⓑ 4' 10"   Ⓔ NG
   Ⓒ 4' 8"

7. The carnival sold 178 ride tickets on Saturday. On Sunday they sold 212 ride tickets. Which is the best estimate for how many tickets they sold in all?

   Ⓐ 450   Ⓓ 300
   Ⓑ 390   Ⓔ NG
   Ⓒ 350

8. Gary is two years older than Seth. Bill is Seth's older brother. Liz is Seth's younger sister. Robin is two years younger than Gary. Which of the following is a reasonable conclusion?

   Ⓐ Bill is older than Gary.
   Ⓑ Seth is older than Robin.
   Ⓒ Liz and Robin are the same age.
   Ⓓ Seth is two years younger than Bill.
   Ⓔ Robin is younger than Bill.

GO ON ▷

9. Dave's dog Oscar usually catches 1 out of every 3 balls that Dave throws him. If Dave throws the ball to Oscar 30 times, about how many will Oscar catch?

   Ⓐ 3   Ⓓ 10
   Ⓑ 6   Ⓔ NG
   Ⓒ 9

10. There are 3 winning ducks in the Duck Pond game at the fair. If there are 24 ducks in all, what is the probability that someone will choose a winning duck with one try?

    Ⓐ $\frac{1}{8}$ Ⓓ $\frac{1}{3}$
    Ⓑ $\frac{3}{12}$ Ⓔ NG
    Ⓒ $\frac{8}{24}$

11. The first time Paige played the video game StarMan she scored 3000 points. The next three times she played she scored 5100 points, 10,440 points, and 13,280 points. What was her average score on StarMan?

    Ⓐ 7670   Ⓓ 7950
    Ⓑ 7770   Ⓔ NG
    Ⓒ 7850

12. Gil borrowed $110 from his parents to buy a bike. So far he has paid back 40% of the money he borrowed. How much money does he have left to pay?

    Ⓐ $66   Ⓓ $4.40
    Ⓑ $44   Ⓔ NG
    Ⓒ $6.60

13. Mrs. Carter bought a coffee table that was marked 20% off. If the original price of the table was $125, how much did she pay for the table?

    Ⓐ $20   Ⓒ $100   Ⓔ NG
    Ⓑ $25   Ⓓ $120

14. Dana has a coupon worth 25% off any sandwich at Subs and Stuff when you buy a large drink for $1.09. If Dana buys a large drink and a sandwich that usually costs $3.40, how much will she pay?

    Ⓐ $.85   Ⓒ $2.55   Ⓔ NG
    Ⓑ $1.94   Ⓓ $3.64

15. One box of brownie mix makes 18 brownies. One package of muffin mix makes 12 muffins. How many muffins and brownies can Louie make in all with 4 boxes of brownie mix and 3 packages of muffin mix?

    Ⓐ 210   Ⓒ 102   Ⓔ NG
    Ⓑ 108   Ⓓ 88

16. Dan's parents are planning to drive cross-country. Which information is NOT needed to figure out how often they will have to stop for gas and how much the gas for the whole trip will cost?

    Ⓐ how many hours they want to drive each day
    Ⓑ how much gas costs per gallon
    Ⓒ how many miles per gallon their car gets
    Ⓓ how many miles they plan to drive
    Ⓔ how many gallons their tank holds

STOP

Number Correct/Total = _____ /16

Solving Equations and Inequalities

Solving equations and inequalities; plotting points on a graph

Directions: Choose the best answer for each question.

A If $565 + x = 890$, then $x =$

 Ⓐ 325   Ⓓ 1455

 Ⓑ 335   Ⓔ NG

 Ⓒ 1355

B If $x \div 5 > 20$, then:

 Ⓐ $x > 100$ Ⓓ $x < 100$

 Ⓑ $x \div 20 < 5$ Ⓔ NG

 Ⓒ $20\, x > 120$

Example A asks you to solve an equation by finding the unknown number that makes the sentence true. In Example A, the equation may be read: 565 plus a number x equals 890. To find x, the unknown number, you must get it by itself on one side of the equation. To do this, subtract 565 from both sides of the equation, as shown below.

$$\begin{array}{rrr} 565 + & x = & 890 \\ -565 & & -565 \\ \hline & x = & 325 \end{array}$$
890 − 565 = 325, and the number 325 makes the sentence true. 565 + 325 = 890. Choice Ⓐ is correct.

Example B asks you to solve an inequality. To do this, first set up the problem as an equation:

$$\begin{array}{r} x \div 5 = 20 \\ (5) \quad (5) \\ x = 100 \end{array}$$
Then solve the equation. Multiply both sides of the equation by 5, as shown. 20 × 5 = 100, so $x = 100$.

If $x = 100$ when $x \div 5 = 20$, then x must be greater than 100 when $x \div 5 > 100$. Choice Ⓐ is correct.

Now look at some example test questions about graphing on page 126.

Directions: Look at the coordinate graph below. Use it to answer the questions.

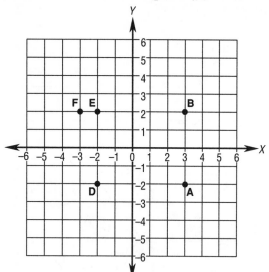

C What point is located at (3,2)?

Ⓐ A   Ⓓ F

Ⓑ B   Ⓔ NG

Ⓒ E

D Where is point D located?

Ⓐ (2,2)   Ⓓ (−2,−2)

Ⓑ (2,−2)   Ⓔ NG

Ⓒ (−2,2)

These questions are about finding or plotting points on a coordinate graph. Think of a graph as two number lines which cross each other at zero.

To find the answer to Example C, read the points on the graph. These points are called **coordinates**. The coordinates are given as two numbers in parentheses, as in (3,2). The first number is always on the **x-axis**, which is the horizontal line. (To find positive numbers, go to the right; for negative numbers, go to the left.) The second number is on the **y-axis**, which is the vertical line (positive numbers up, negative numbers down). To find (3,2), go over three points to the right and up 2 points. The point at (3,2) is point B. Choice Ⓑ is correct.

To answer Example D, you must find the coordinates for point D. Find point D, then count up to the x-axis. The first coordinate is −2. Then count to the right to the y-axis. Point D is at −2 on the y-axis. This gives you the second coordinate of your ordered pair. Point D is located at the coordinates (−2,−2). Choice Ⓓ is correct.

Test-Taking Tips

1 Remember that an equation must stay balanced. If you subtract a number from one side, you must also subtract it from the other side (as in Example A).

2 Solve an equation or inequality by first getting the unknown number (x or n, for example) by itself on one side of the equation.

3 When reading coordinates on a graph, remember that the first number goes across, to the left or right, and the second number goes up or down (as in Example C).

Go for it

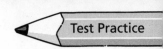

Test Practice 7: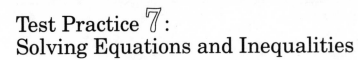
Solving Equations and Inequalities

Time: **16** minutes

Directions: Choose the best answer for each question.

1. If $98 + x = 159$, then $x =$

   Ⓐ 51   Ⓓ 257
   Ⓑ 52   Ⓔ NG
   Ⓒ 61

2. If $\frac{3}{20} = \frac{6}{x}$, then $x =$

   Ⓐ 18   Ⓓ 120
   Ⓑ 40   Ⓔ NG
   Ⓒ 60

3. If $x - 39 = 77$, then $x =$

   Ⓐ 116   Ⓓ 36
   Ⓑ 106   Ⓔ NG
   Ⓒ 38

4. If $x = 6$, then $330x =$

   Ⓐ 55   Ⓓ 1990
   Ⓑ 324   Ⓔ NG
   Ⓒ 1880

5. If $x = 3$, then $9x - 7 =$

   Ⓐ 6   Ⓓ 27
   Ⓑ 11   Ⓔ NG
   Ⓒ 20

6. If x is a positive whole number and $\frac{3}{2} = \frac{x}{24}$, then $x =$

   Ⓐ 8   Ⓓ 2
   Ⓑ 6   Ⓔ NG
   Ⓒ 4

7. If $x + 2 < 9$, then:

   Ⓐ $x > 7$ Ⓓ $x < 7$
   Ⓑ $x > 9$ Ⓔ NG
   Ⓒ $x < 2$

8. If $25x > 100$, then:

   Ⓐ $x > 4$ Ⓓ $x > 5$
   Ⓑ $x < 100$ Ⓔ NG
   Ⓒ $x < 25$

9. If $\frac{x}{9} < \frac{1}{3}$, then:

   Ⓐ $x < 27$ Ⓓ $x > 3$
   Ⓑ $x < 3$ Ⓔ NG
   Ⓒ $x > 12$

10. If $x + 10 > 30$, then:

    Ⓐ $x > 20$ Ⓓ $x < 40$
    Ⓑ $x > 3$ Ⓔ NG
    Ⓒ $x < 20$

11. If $x + 3 > 3x - 1$, then:

    Ⓐ $x < 1$ Ⓓ $x < 2$
    Ⓑ $x > 1$ Ⓔ NG
    Ⓒ $x > 2$

12. If $16 - 2x > 4 + x$, then:

    Ⓐ $x > 3$ Ⓓ $x > 12$
    Ⓑ $x < 4$ Ⓔ NG
    Ⓒ $x < 2$

 GO ON

Use the coordinate graph to answer questions 13–16.

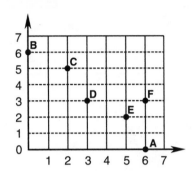

13. What point is at (6,0)?

    (A) A   (D) F
    (B) B   (E) NG
    (C) D

14. Where is point C located?

    (A) (5,2)   (D) (2,5)
    (B) (5,5)   (E) NG
    (C) (2,4)

15. Which point is at (3,3)?

    (A) B   (D) F
    (B) D   (E) NG
    (C) E

16. Where would point F be located if you moved it 1 unit to the left and 1 unit up?

    (A) (6,3)   (D) (5,4)
    (B) (2,4)   (E) NG
    (C) (4,5)

Use the coordinate graph to answer questions 17–20.

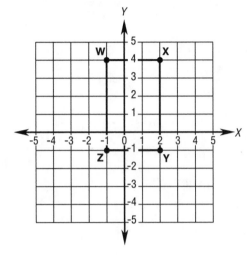

17. Where is point W located?

    (A) (2,4)   (D) (4,2)
    (B) (−1,4)   (E) NG
    (C) (1,4)

18. What will be the coordinates of point Y if you slide rectangle WXYZ up 1 unit?

    (A) (2,−1)   (D) (2,−2)
    (B) (0,2)   (E) NG
    (C) (2,1)

19. How many units to the left would you have to move rectangle WXYZ to make the coordinates of point Z (−4,−1)?

    (A) 4   (D) 1
    (B) 3   (E) NG
    (C) 2

20. If you moved rectangle WXYZ down 2 units and to the right 2 units, where would point X be located?

    (A) (4,2)   (D) (2,4)
    (B) (3,1)   (E) NG
    (C) (2,2)

STOP

Number Correct/Total = _____ /20

Geometric Figures

Recognizing geometric figures and their features

Directions: Choose the best answer for each question.

A If figure ABCD is congruent to figure WXYZ, then $\overline{AB}$ is congruent to —

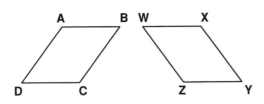

ⓐ $\overline{WX}$ ⓓ $\overline{ZW}$
ⓑ $\overline{XY}$ ⓔ NG
ⓒ $\overline{YZ}$

B Which triangle is isosceles?

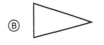

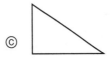

Example A gives two congruent figures. **Congruent figures** have exactly the same size and shape. There is a rule in geometry that says that corresponding sides of congruent figures are congruent. In Example A, then, you must find the side of figure WXYZ that corresponds to $\overline{AB}$ in figure ABCD. If you flip WXYZ over, you will see that $\overline{YZ}$ corresponds to, and so is congruent to, $\overline{AB}$. Choice ⓒ is correct.

Example B asks you to identify an isosceles triangle. An **isosceles triangle** has two equal sides. Look at the triangles in Example B. Which one has two equal sides? The triangle in choice ⓑ has two equal sides, so it is an isosceles triangle.

Now let's look at some more test question examples on page 130.

C What is the circumference of the circle below? (Use π = 3.14)

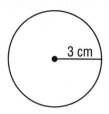

3 cm

- Ⓐ 6 cm
- Ⓑ 9.42 cm
- Ⓒ 18 cm
- Ⓓ 18.84 cm
- Ⓔ NG

D What is the volume of this container?

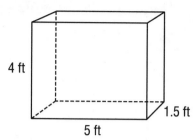

4 ft
1.5 ft
5 ft

- Ⓐ 10.5 cu ft
- Ⓑ 20 cu ft
- Ⓒ 21.5 cu ft
- Ⓓ 30 cu ft
- Ⓔ NG

These examples are about measuring geometric figures. In Example C, the question asks you to find the circumference of the circle, given that the radius is 3 cm. To find the **circumference** of a circle, use the formula $c = 2\pi r$ (where c = circumference and r = radius). In Example C, 2 × 3.14 (π) × 3 (radius) = 18.84. The circumference is 18.84, so choice Ⓓ is correct.

In Example D, you must find the volume of the container. **Volume** is the amount of space taken up by a solid figure. To find the volume (v) of a container, multiply *length × width × height*. In Example D, 5 ft (l) × 1.5 ft (w) × 4 ft (h) = 30 cubic feet. Choice Ⓓ is correct.

Math Pointers

To find...	Use this formula...	
Perimeter of a rectangle	$p = 2l + 2w$	(l = length; w = width)
Circumference of a circle	$c = 2\pi r$	(π = 3.14; r = radius)
Area of a rectangle	$a = l \times w$	(l = length; w = width)
Area of a triangle	$a = \frac{1}{2}b \times h$	(b = base; h = height)
Area of a circle	$a = 2\pi d$	(d = diameter)
Volume of a rectangular prism	$v = l \times w \times h$	(l = length; w = width)

Test-Taking Tips

1 Look for key words and numbers to help you find the answers. (In Example C, the key word is *circumference*, and the key number is *3 cm*.)

2 Study the diagrams and figures carefully to find the information you need. Draw your own pictures if they will help you answer the questions.

3 Write down the formula that you should use to solve each measurement problem, then plug in the numbers from the problem.

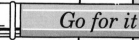

Go for it

Test Practice 8: Geometric Figures

Time: 12 minutes

Directions: Choose the best answer for each question.

1. Figure 1 is congruent to Figure 2. Which side of figure 2 is congruent to $\overline{EA}$ in Figure 1?

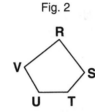

Fig. 1   Fig. 2

Ⓐ $\overline{VR}$ Ⓓ $\overline{TU}$
Ⓑ $\overline{ST}$ Ⓔ $\overline{RS}$
Ⓒ $\overline{UV}$

2. Which point is the vertex of $\angle GFH$?

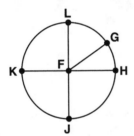

Ⓐ F   Ⓓ K
Ⓑ G   Ⓔ J
Ⓒ H

3. Which figure has an X on a face?

Ⓐ   Ⓓ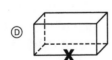

Ⓑ   Ⓔ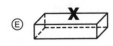

Ⓒ

4. Which is a right triangle?

Ⓐ   Ⓓ

Ⓑ   Ⓔ

Ⓒ

5. Which is an equilateral triangle?

Ⓐ   Ⓓ

Ⓑ   Ⓔ

Ⓒ

6. Which line appears to be perpendicular to AB?

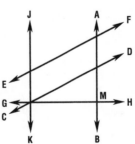

Ⓐ CD   Ⓓ JK
Ⓑ EF   Ⓔ MD
Ⓒ GH

7. Which is parallel to $\overline{HJ}$?

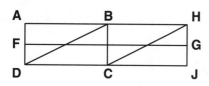

   Ⓐ $\overline{AB}$ Ⓒ $\overline{FG}$ Ⓔ $\overline{BC}$

   Ⓑ $\overline{CH}$ Ⓓ $\overline{DB}$

8. Which angle measures about 45°?

  Ⓐ   Ⓓ

  Ⓑ   Ⓔ

  Ⓒ

9. Which is an obtuse angle?

  Ⓐ   Ⓓ

  Ⓑ   Ⓔ

  Ⓒ

10. What is the circumference of this circle? (π = 3.14)

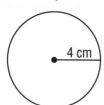

4 cm

  Ⓐ 12.12 cm   Ⓓ 25.12 cm

  Ⓑ 12.56 cm   Ⓔ NG

  Ⓒ 24.12 cm

11. What is the perimeter of this figure?

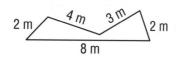

4 m 3 m 2 m 2 m 8 m

  Ⓐ 16 m   Ⓒ 19 m   Ⓔ NG

  Ⓑ 18 m   Ⓓ 20 m

12. The area of a square ABCD is 16 sq in. How long is each side?

  Ⓐ 2 in   Ⓓ 32 in

  Ⓑ 4 in   Ⓔ NG

  Ⓒ 8 in

13. What is the area of a rectangular park that is 42 yards long and 19 yards wide?

  Ⓐ 61 sq yd   Ⓓ 898 sq yd

  Ⓑ 122 sq yd   Ⓔ NG

  Ⓒ 796 sq yd

14. What is the volume of the box below?

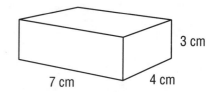

3 cm 7 cm 4 cm

  Ⓐ 14 cm^3 Ⓓ 84 cm^3

  Ⓑ 28 cm^3 Ⓔ NG

  Ⓒ 74 cm^3

15. Mia has a rectangular bucket that is 1.5 feet tall, .75 feet wide and 1 foot long. How much water will her bucket hold?

  Ⓐ 32.5 cu ft   Ⓓ 1.125 cu ft

  Ⓑ 11.25 cu ft   Ⓔ NG

  Ⓒ 3.25 cu ft

16. Which of these statements would prove that triangle DEF is a right triangle?

  Ⓐ $\overline{DE} = \overline{DF}$ Ⓓ $\angle E > \angle F$

  Ⓑ $\overline{DF} > \overline{DE}$ Ⓔ NG

  Ⓒ $\angle E = 90°$

STOP

Number Correct/Total = _____ /16

Measurement

Using metric and standard measures, telling time, and estimating

Directions: Choose the best answer for each question.

A Jill went to the library at 9:30 on Saturday morning. She spent 2 hours working on a report for school. On the way home, Jill spent $1\frac{1}{2}$ hours having lunch at Terri's. What time did Jill leave Terri's?

   Ⓐ 12:30 p.m.   Ⓒ 1:30 p.m.

   Ⓑ 1:00 p.m.   Ⓓ 2:00 p.m.

To answer Example A, you have to figure out how much time has passed, then add it to 9:30. You can solve this problem by picturing or drawing clocks.

9:30   +   2 hours   +   1 hour, 30 minutes

You can also figure out the problem in another way. Jill spent 2 hours at the library and $1\frac{1}{2}$ hours at lunch, for a total of $3\frac{1}{2}$ hours. If you add 3 hours, 30 minutes to 9:30, you get 12:60, which is 1:00 o'clock. Choice Ⓑ is correct.

Example A deals with time. The examples below deal with measurement of length and conversion between the **metric** and **standard systems** of measure.

B Jed is 1.58 meters tall. How many centimeters tall is he?

   Ⓐ .158 cm   Ⓒ 158.0 cm

   Ⓑ 15.8 cm   Ⓓ 1580.0 cm

C Letty drove 200 kilometers yesterday. About how many miles did she drive?

   Ⓐ 100 mi   Ⓒ 140 mi

   Ⓑ 120 mi   Ⓓ 320 mi

Example B deals with the metric system of measurement. You must convert meters to centimeters. 1 meter = 100 centimeters, so 1.58 × 100 = 158 cm. Choice Ⓒ is correct.

To solve Example C, you must convert from kilometers to miles. 1 kilometer = .62 miles, so you can solve the problem by multiplying: 200 km × .62 = 124 miles. The question asks *about* how many miles she drove, so choice Ⓑ is correct. 120 miles is closest to the exact number of 124.

TO MONTREAL
200 KM
124 MI

Math Pointers

Metric System

Weight
- 1 kilogram (kg) = 1,000 grams (g)
- 1 metric ton = 1,000 kg

Length
- 1 kilometer (km) = 1,000 meters (m)
- 1 m = 100 centimeters (cm) = 1,000 millimeters (mm)

Volume Capacity
- 1 kiloliter (kl) = 1,000 liters (l)
- 1 liter (l) = 100 centiliters (cl) = 1,000 milliliters (ml)

Metric to Standard

Conversions
- 1 kg = 2.2 lb
- 1 m = 1.1 yd
- 1 km = .62 miles
- 1 l = .88 qt

Standard System

Weight
- 16 ounces (oz) = 1 pound (lb)
- 2,000 lb = 1 ton

Length
- 1 foot (ft) = 12 inches (in)
- 1 yard (yd) = 3 ft = 36 in
- 1 mile = 1,760 yd = 5,280 ft

Volume Capacity
- 1 cup = 8 oz
- 1 pint (pt) = 2 cups = 16 oz
- 1 quart (qt) = 2 pt = 32 oz
- 1 gallon (gal) = 4 qt = 128 oz

Standard to Metric

Conversions
- 1 lb = 454 g
- 1 in = 2.54 cm
- 1 mile = 1.6 km
- 1 qt = .95 l

Test-Taking Tips

1 Look for key words and numbers in each question to make sure you know what you have to find. (In Example A, the key words are *what time*. The key numbers are *9:30, 2 hours*, and *1½ hours*. In Example C, key words are *kilometers*, *miles*, and *about how many*.)

2 Get to know the units of measurement in both the metric and standard systems, and how to convert from one system to another.

Go for it

Test Practice ⑨: Measurement

Time: **15** minutes

Directions: Choose the best answer for each question.

1. Wendy read her book for 2 hours, 15 minutes on Thursday night. She stopped reading at 9:30. What time did she begin reading?

   Ⓐ 11:45   © 7:45
   Ⓑ 8:15   Ⓓ 7:15

2. Ryan rode his bike from 10:45 a.m. until 12:30 p.m. How long did he ride?

   Ⓐ 45 minutes
   Ⓑ 1 hour, 15 minutes
   © 1 hour, 45 minutes
   Ⓓ 2 hours, 15 minutes

3. Kelvin's birthday party started at 4:00. It was over 3 hours and 20 minutes later. At what time did the party end?

   Ⓐ 6:40   © 7:20
   Ⓑ 7:10   Ⓓ 7:40

4. It takes Althea an hour and 10 minutes to bake a batch of 3 dozen cookies. If she wants to be finished making cookies by 9:00 to watch a TV show, what is the latest time she can start baking cookies?

   Ⓐ 7:30   © 8:05
   Ⓑ 7:50   Ⓓ 8:10

5. Will got to the mall at 12:00. He spent 30 minutes in the video arcade. Then he spent 25 minutes in the hobby store. Then he spent an hour eating lunch with his friends before going home. What time did he leave the mall?

   Ⓐ 12:25   © 1:25
   Ⓑ 12:35   Ⓓ 1:55

6. A train left Springfield at 8:10 and reached New Haven at 10:15. After a 15-minute stopover, the train left New Haven and reached New York City at 12:05. How long was the trip from New Haven to New York City?

   Ⓐ 1 hour, 35 minutes
   Ⓑ 1 hour, 45 minutes
   © 1 hour, 50 minutes
   Ⓓ 3 hours, 55 minutes

7. Which unit should you use to find out how far it is from Baltimore, Maryland, to Richmond, Virginia?

   Ⓐ kilometer   © centimeter
   Ⓑ meter   Ⓓ kilogram

8. Which unit should you use to find out how much a blue whale weighs?

   Ⓐ pound   © ton
   Ⓑ ounce   Ⓓ pint

9. If you wanted to compare the volume of a paper cup to the volume of a jelly jar, which unit should you use?

   Ⓐ kilogram   © milligram
   Ⓑ liter   Ⓓ milliliter

10. Bart was $5\frac{1}{2}$ feet tall last year. This year he has grown 2 inches. How tall is Bart now?

    Ⓐ 5' 6"   © 5' 10"
    Ⓑ 5' 8"   Ⓓ 6' 2"

11. Ann brought 3 gallons of fruit punch to the class party. She and her classmates drank 6 quarts of punch. How much punch was left?

    Ⓐ $1\frac{1}{2}$ gal   Ⓒ 3 qt

    Ⓑ 1 gal   Ⓓ 2 qt

12. Vince's puppy weighed 5 kilograms when Vince got him. He has gained 500 grams. How much does he weigh now?

    Ⓐ 5.05 kg   Ⓒ 10 kg

    Ⓑ 5.5 kg   Ⓓ 55 kg

13. Becky's bean plant was 21 centimeters tall when she measured it last week in science class. Now it is 21.5 cm tall. How much did it grow?

    Ⓐ .5 m   Ⓒ .5 mm

    Ⓑ 5 cm   Ⓓ 5 mm

14. Marla drove 800 kilometers last week. About how many miles did she drive?

    Ⓐ 500 mi   Ⓒ 800 mi

    Ⓑ 600 mi   Ⓓ 1300 mi

15. Calley weighs 120 pounds. About how many kilograms does she weigh?

    Ⓐ 260 kg   Ⓒ 75 kg

    Ⓑ 100 kg   Ⓓ 55 kg

16. Diana weighs about 3 times as much as her little sister. If Diana weighs about 89 pounds, about how much does her sister weigh?

    Ⓐ 25 lb   Ⓒ 30 lb

    Ⓑ 26 lb   Ⓓ 33 lb

17. Mr. Ritter has a ladder with 4 sections. Each section is 3.6 feet long. About how tall will Mr. Ritter's ladder be if he extends it to its full height?

    Ⓐ 12 ft   Ⓒ 16 ft

    Ⓑ 14 ft   Ⓓ 18 ft

18. There are 3 rooms along the front of the Chungs' house. The living room is about 4.1 meters long. Each of the bedrooms is about 2.8 meters long. About how long is the front of the house?

    Ⓐ 9–10 m   Ⓒ 6–7 m

    Ⓑ 7–8 m   Ⓓ 4–5 m

19. A cubic yard of gravel weighs about 6000 pounds, and a dumptruck carries 9 cu yd per load. About how many tons does a truckload of gravel weigh?

    Ⓐ 54,000 tons   Ⓒ 27 tons

    Ⓑ 27,000 tons   Ⓓ 9 tons

20. If the mass of 2 golf balls is 98 grams, the mass of 3 golf balls would be about —

    Ⓐ 200 g   Ⓒ 160 g

    Ⓑ 180 g   Ⓓ 150 g

Number Correct/Total = _____ /20

Interpreting Data

Reading and interpreting tables, charts, and graphs

Directions: The graph below shows the number of pairs of roller skates sold by Skates, Etc. between 1980 and 1990. Use the graph to answer each question.

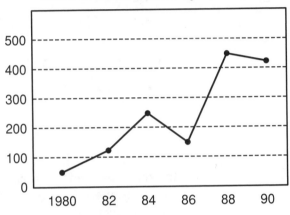

Sales of Roller Skates by Skates, Etc.

A How many more pairs of roller skates were sold in 1984 than in 1982?

   Ⓐ 100   Ⓒ 150

   Ⓑ 125   Ⓓ 175

B Between which years did roller skating most likely experience a large increase in popularity?

   Ⓐ 1980–1982   Ⓒ 1984–1986

   Ⓑ 1982–1984   Ⓓ 1986–1988

     To answer Example A, find the year 1984 on the graph. Follow up to the graph line. Then find the number at the left side of the graph that corresponds to the level of the graph line. Note that 250 pairs of skates were sold in 1984. Now repeat the process for 1982. You will find that 125 pairs of skates were sold that year. To find the difference, subtract: 250 − 125 = 125. Choice Ⓑ is correct.

     Example B asks you to make an **inference** from the information presented in the graph. It is likely that a sharp increase in the sales of roller skates indicates an increase in the popularity of roller skating. For the two-year periods on this graph, the largest increase in sales occurred between 1986 and 1988. Roller skating probably became suddenly more popular during those years. Choice Ⓓ is correct.

Test-Taking Tips

1 Look for the key words in each question such as *most, least, how many, more than, less than, in all.* (In Example A, the key words are *how many.* In Example B, the key word is *increase.*)

2 Look back at the chart, table, or graph to answer each question.

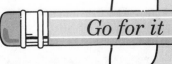

Go for it

Test Practice 10 : Interpreting Data

Time: **10** minutes

Questions 1–3. The table below shows the driving mileage between cities. Use the table to answer each question.

Mileage Table

City	Lee	Riley	Suma	Vista	Ware
Lee	x	48	110	94	33
Riley	48	x	100	96	40
Suma	110	100	x	61	78
Vista	94	96	61	x	52
Ware	33	40	78	52	x

1. How many miles is it from Vista to Suma?

    ⓐ 110   © 96

    ⓑ 100   ⓓ 61

2. If you traveled from Riley to Lee, how many miles would you travel?

    ⓐ 40   © 96

    ⓑ 48   ⓓ 100

3. Which two cities are closest together?

    ⓐ Riley and Suma

    ⓑ Vista and Suma

    © Ware and Lee

    ⓓ Vista and Ware

Questions 4–6. The bar graph below shows the number of bushels of oranges and grapefruit produced by a small farm in different years. Use the graph to answer each question.

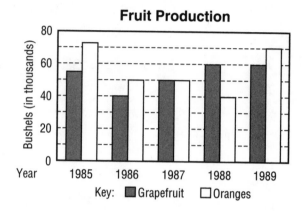

4. In what year did the farm produce the same number of bushels of grapefruit and oranges?

    ⓐ 1986   © 1988

    ⓑ 1987   ⓓ 1989

5. How many more bushels of oranges than grapefruit did the farm produce in 1985?

    ⓐ 15,000   © 20,000

    ⓑ 17,500   ⓓ 25,000

6. Which year had the greatest difference between the production of grapefruit and oranges?

    ⓐ 1985   © 1988

    ⓑ 1986   ⓓ 1989

Questions 7–9. The circle graph below shows the breakdown of a region's economy by type of activity. Use the graph to answer each question.

ECONOMIC ACTIVITY

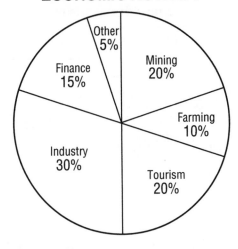

7. Which activity makes up the largest percentage of the economy?

   Ⓐ industry   Ⓒ mining

   Ⓑ farming   Ⓓ finance

8. What percentage of the region's economy is made up of mining interests?

   Ⓐ 15%   Ⓒ 25%

   Ⓑ 20%   Ⓓ 30%

9. Which two activities together make up one-quarter of the economy?

   Ⓐ finance and mining

   Ⓑ farming and tourism

   Ⓒ mining and industry

   Ⓓ farming and finance

Questions 10–12. The chart below provides information about several cities in the United States. Use the chart to answer each question.

U.S. Cities

City	Population (1980)	Average Yearly Precipitation
Atlanta	425,022	48 in
Boston	562,994	43 in
Chicago	3,005,078	33 in
Denver	492,365	16 in
Houston	1,595,167	45 in
Los Angeles	2,966,850	14 in
Miami	346,865	58 in

10. Which is the driest city, on average?

    Ⓐ Miami   Ⓒ Los Angeles

    Ⓑ Houston   Ⓓ Chicago

11. On the average, how much more precipitation does Boston receive than Denver each year?

    Ⓐ 5 in   Ⓒ 16 in

    Ⓑ 11 in   Ⓓ 27 in

12. Approximately how many more people lived in Boston in 1980 than in Atlanta?

    Ⓐ 100,000   Ⓒ 180,000

    Ⓑ 140,000   Ⓓ 220,000

STOP

Number Correct/Total = _____ /12

*This test will tell you how well you might score on a standardized math test **after** using this book. If you compare your scores on Tryout Tests 1 and 2, you'll see how much you've learned!*

Math Tryout Test 2

Time: **40** minutes

Directions: Choose the best answer for each question. Fill in the circle beside your answer. The answer to the sample question (**S**) has been filled in for you.

S What is the value of the 1 in 3,215,687?

Ⓐ 1,000,000
Ⓑ 100,000
● 10,000
Ⓓ 1000

1. Which number is expressed by

$$(5 \times 10^4) + (2 \times 10^3) + (6 \times 10^2)$$?

Ⓐ 520,600
Ⓑ 52,600
Ⓒ 5260
Ⓓ 526

2. Which is a prime number?

Ⓐ 38   Ⓒ 57
Ⓑ 49   Ⓓ 67

3. What are the prime factors of 45?

Ⓐ $3 \times 3 \times 5$
Ⓑ 9×5
Ⓒ $5 \times 2 \times 3$
Ⓓ 15×3

4. What is the square root of 196?

Ⓐ 98   Ⓒ 14
Ⓑ 49   Ⓓ 7

5. Which number fits in the box?

$$(9 \times 3) + (9 \times 12) + (9 \times 14) = 9 \times \square$$

Ⓐ 29   Ⓒ 98
Ⓑ 36   Ⓓ 134

6. What is $\frac{16}{36}$ in its simplest form?

Ⓐ $\frac{1}{3}$ Ⓒ $\frac{1}{2}$
Ⓑ $\frac{4}{9}$ Ⓓ $\frac{8}{18}$

7. Which fraction is another name for .40?

Ⓐ $\frac{1}{2}$ Ⓒ $\frac{3}{5}$
Ⓑ $\frac{8}{10}$ Ⓓ $\frac{2}{5}$

8. What is $\frac{3}{4}$ expressed as a percent?

Ⓐ .75%   Ⓒ 75%
Ⓑ 7.5%   Ⓓ 750%

9. What is the value of the 7 in .1874?

Ⓐ $\frac{70}{1}$ Ⓒ $\frac{70}{1000}$
Ⓑ $\frac{7}{10}$ Ⓓ $\frac{7}{1000}$

10. What is 54.45 rounded to the nearest whole number?

Ⓐ 54   Ⓒ 54.5
Ⓑ 54.4   Ⓓ 55

GO ON

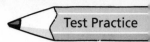

11.

97890
− 4598

Ⓐ 93,202
Ⓑ 93,292
Ⓒ 93,382
Ⓓ 93,392
Ⓔ NG

12.

472
× 68

Ⓐ 31,096
Ⓑ 31,596
Ⓒ 32,086
Ⓓ 32,096
Ⓔ NG

13.

$6\frac{2}{3}$
$+ 4\frac{4}{5}$

Ⓐ $10\frac{1}{3}$
Ⓑ $10\frac{2}{15}$
Ⓒ $10\frac{3}{4}$
Ⓓ $11\frac{7}{15}$
Ⓔ NG

14.

$\frac{6}{7} \div \frac{1}{3} =$

Ⓐ $2\frac{3}{7}$
Ⓑ $2\frac{2}{7}$
Ⓒ $\frac{6}{21}$
Ⓓ $\frac{3}{7}$
Ⓔ NG

15.

33.45
× .60

Ⓐ .2007
Ⓑ 2.007
Ⓒ 20.07
Ⓓ 200.7
Ⓔ NG

16. 24 is what percent of 40?

Ⓐ 35
Ⓑ 40
Ⓒ 55
Ⓓ 60
Ⓔ NG

17. Craig got scores of 77, 88, 100, 91, and 89 on a series of tests. What was Craig's median score on the tests?

Ⓐ 88
Ⓑ 89
Ⓒ 90
Ⓓ 100
Ⓔ NG

18. What is the probability of spinning "Lose Turn" on the first spin?

Ⓐ $\frac{1}{6}$
Ⓑ $\frac{1}{5}$
Ⓒ $\frac{1}{4}$
Ⓓ $\frac{1}{3}$
Ⓔ NG

19. Carol got a package of 12 hair bands for $2.28. How much was each hair band ?

Ⓐ $.12
Ⓑ $.19
Ⓒ $1.19
Ⓓ $1.90
Ⓔ NG

20. Ken drove 128 miles in $2\frac{1}{2}$ hours. What was his average speed during the trip?

Ⓐ 52 mph
Ⓑ 51.5 mph
Ⓒ 51.2 mph
Ⓓ 51 mph
Ⓔ NG

 GO ON

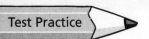
Math Tryout Test 2 (continued)

21. Val missed 2 out of 12 questions on the first half of the math test. On the second half of the test, she missed 3 out of 8 questions. What percent of the total questions did she get right?

   Ⓐ 25%   Ⓓ 80%

   Ⓑ 40%   Ⓔ NG

   Ⓒ 75%

22. Dale has a 20% discount coupon for Games World. If he buys a computer game originally priced at $32.00, how much will he have to pay?

   Ⓐ $6.40   Ⓓ $25.60

   Ⓑ $8.00   Ⓔ NG

   Ⓒ $24.00

23. At the Dole School, there are 30 students in each class, and 28 of the 30 buy their lunch each day. At the same rate, how many of the students in 8 classes would buy their lunch?

   Ⓐ 220   Ⓓ 240

   Ⓑ 224   Ⓔ NG

   Ⓒ 228

24. Abby ordered a $19 pair of pants from the J.J. Wear catalog. She had seen the same pants for sale at Maxi's for $24.95. She also ordered 2 belts for $5.00 each and a scarf on sale for $11.00. What information is NOT needed to find the total cost of Abby's order?

   Ⓐ Her pants were $19.00.

   Ⓑ The belts were $5.00 each.

   Ⓒ The scarf was on sale for $11.00.

   Ⓓ Her blouse was $20.00.

   Ⓔ The same pants cost $24.95 at Maxi's.

25. If $\frac{20}{x} = \frac{3}{10}$, then $x =$

   Ⓐ 60   Ⓒ 20   Ⓔ NG

   Ⓑ 30   Ⓓ 6

26. If $x + 18 > 45 - 9$, then:

   Ⓐ $x < 14$ Ⓒ $x > 18$ Ⓔ NG

   Ⓑ $x < 16$ Ⓓ $x > 34$

27. If $8x > 6$, then x must be $>$

   Ⓐ $\frac{2}{3}$ Ⓒ 2   Ⓔ NG

   Ⓑ $\frac{3}{4}$ Ⓓ 14

Use the graph to answer questions 28–30.

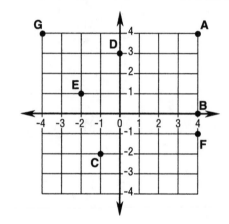

28. Which point is at (4,4)?

   Ⓐ A   Ⓒ D   Ⓔ NG

   Ⓑ B   Ⓓ F

29. Where is point C located?

   Ⓐ (−2,−1)   Ⓒ (−1,−2)   Ⓔ NG

   Ⓑ (1,2)   Ⓓ (−1,2)

30. Which point is located on the x-axis?

   Ⓐ G   Ⓒ E   Ⓔ NG

   Ⓑ F   Ⓓ B

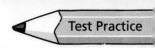

31. How many faces does the figure below have?

Ⓐ 3

Ⓑ 4

Ⓒ 6

Ⓓ 8

Ⓔ NG

32. Which is a scalene triangle?

Ⓐ

Ⓑ

Ⓒ

Ⓓ

Ⓔ

33. Which is perpendicular to AB at point P?

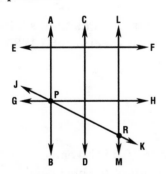

Ⓐ CD

Ⓑ EF

Ⓒ GH

Ⓓ JK

Ⓔ LM

34. Which of these angles measures 180°?

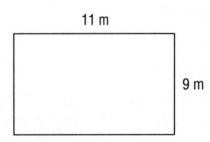

35. What is the circumference of the circle below? ($\pi = 3.14$)

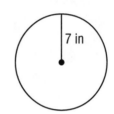

7 in

Ⓐ 21.91 in

Ⓑ 21.96 in

Ⓒ 43.86 in

Ⓓ 43.96 in

Ⓔ NG

36. What is the area of this rectangle?

11 m

9 m

Ⓐ 20 m²

Ⓑ 40 m²

Ⓒ 90 m²

Ⓓ 99 m²

Ⓔ NG

GO ON

Math Tryout Test 2 (continued)

37. Kelly has a square cooler that measures 34 inches by 15 inches by 24 inches. How many cubic inches of water will her cooler hold if it is full?

   Ⓐ 73 cu in   Ⓓ 12,140 cu in

   Ⓑ 816 cu in   Ⓔ NG

   Ⓒ 11,640 cu in

38. Brian spent 40 minutes at a tutoring session after school. Then he went to basketball practice for $1\frac{1}{2}$ hours. If he got out of school at 3:00, what time did he finish practice?

   Ⓐ 4:40   Ⓒ 5:10

   Ⓑ 4:50   Ⓓ 5:20

39. Helen needs to buy enough hamburger to feed 18 people. Which unit of measurement would be best to use when she figures out how much hamburger to buy?

   Ⓐ milligram   Ⓒ gram

   Ⓑ kilogram   Ⓓ liter

40. Sam had three 2-liter bottles of soda water. He and his friends drank 250 milliliters of soda. How much soda did Sam have left?

   Ⓐ 575 ml   Ⓒ 5750 ml

   Ⓑ 585 ml   Ⓓ 6750 ml

Questions 41–44. This graph shows the change in the numbers of eagles and falcons in a bird sanctuary over 20 years.

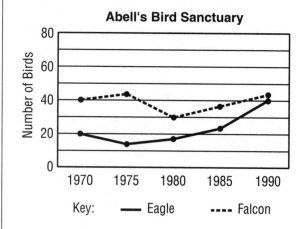

41. How many eagles were there in 1970?

   Ⓐ 15   Ⓒ 20

   Ⓑ 17   Ⓓ 40

42. Between which years did the number of falcons decline?

   Ⓐ 1970–1975   Ⓒ 1980–1985

   Ⓑ 1975–1980   Ⓓ 1985–1990

43. How many more falcons than eagles lived in the bird sanctuary in 1985?

   Ⓐ 4   Ⓒ 14

   Ⓑ 8   Ⓓ 18

44. After what year did the eagles most successfully adapt to their new environment?

   Ⓐ 1970   Ⓒ 1980

   Ⓑ 1975   Ⓓ 1985

Number Correct/Total = _____ /44

Some Things Parents Want To Know About Standardized Tests

Why are national standardized tests sometimes called "high stakes" tests?

Your child's test scores are often used to "track" him or her into a particular educational program. If a child scores well, opportunities for special programs and teachers frequently become available. If scores are low, the child may be marked as a slow student and placed in a program or group that limits the chance to develop. Elementary school standardized tests can actually shape a child's high school program —as well as affect chances for a college education. These are "high stakes" indeed!

How will this book help my child get better test scores?

It will help your child in two ways: one, all the test questions in this study guide focus *exclusively* on the very same skills and content areas tested by the five most widely used standardized tests—your child will learn exactly what he or she needs to know to get better test scores. Two, this study guide provides intensive practice in important and effective test-taking strategies.

How often are national standardized tests given at my child's school?

Most schools give national standardized tests yearly. Usually, they are given in the spring or fall—and in some schools both times. Check with your school to get your child's test dates.

What are standardized tests used for?

The tests are designed to measure the effectiveness of your child's school, and at the same time to identify your child's strengths and weaknesses in reading, language arts, and math. The school's scores can help you learn how well your school is teaching these subjects compared to other schools around the nation and other schools in your own school district.

Why does this book span two grade levels?

Each of the five national standardized tests on which this study guide is based covers two grade levels. It is possible that your child will encounter questions in this guide and on the standardized test that cover content he or she has not yet had. Not to worry: this study guide can provide advance preparation for the content your child will be required to know later this year or next year. Moreover, your child's scores on the standardized tests are adjusted to reflect his or her actual grade level. In any case, the national tests do not expect 100% correct answers or 100% completion of all the test questions—and you needn't either.

When should my child start using this book?

Using this book throughout the school year can be very helpful, since classroom teachers give tests on an average of three out of every five school days. To prepare for the national standardized test covering reading, language arts, and math, spend a few hours each week for about six to eight weeks before the test date.

Should I expect my child to work independently in this book?

This guide is designed for independent study. However, some children may need help getting started, so you'll want to get familiar with the guide's format and content. You'll probably want to show your child how this study guide can help. Work together to set up a regular, and realistic, study schedule. It is important to allow your child to self-score all the tests. This encourages the child to take responsibility for his or her progress and builds confidence that will carry over to school work.

Answer Keys

Reading Tryout Test 1

page 9

1.	Ⓑ	7.	Ⓒ
2.	Ⓒ	8.	Ⓑ
3.	Ⓐ	9.	Ⓑ
4.	Ⓓ	10.	Ⓐ
5.	Ⓒ	11.	Ⓓ
6.	Ⓐ		

page 10

12.	Ⓐ	17.	Ⓓ
13.	Ⓑ	18.	Ⓑ
14.	Ⓒ	19.	Ⓐ
15.	Ⓓ	20.	Ⓓ
16.	Ⓒ	21.	Ⓓ

page 11

22.	Ⓒ	24.	Ⓑ
23.	Ⓓ	25.	Ⓐ

pages 12–13

26.	Ⓐ	31.	Ⓓ
27.	Ⓑ	32.	Ⓓ
28.	Ⓑ	33.	Ⓒ
29.	Ⓓ	34.	Ⓐ
30.	Ⓒ	35.	Ⓑ

Test Practice 1
Word Meaning

page 15

1.	Ⓓ	7.	Ⓓ
2.	Ⓐ	8.	Ⓒ
3.	Ⓓ	9	Ⓑ
4.	Ⓑ	10.	Ⓐ
5.	Ⓒ	11.	Ⓒ
6.	Ⓐ	12.	Ⓐ

Test Practice 2
Word Analysis

page 17

1.	Ⓓ	7.	Ⓑ
2.	Ⓑ	8.	Ⓒ
3.	Ⓒ	9	Ⓑ
4.	Ⓒ	10.	Ⓐ
5.	Ⓓ	11.	Ⓓ
6.	Ⓐ	12.	Ⓑ

Test Practice 3
Synonyms and Antonyms

page 19

1.	Ⓑ	7.	Ⓒ
2.	Ⓓ	8.	Ⓑ
3.	Ⓐ	9.	Ⓐ
4.	Ⓑ	10.	Ⓑ
5.	Ⓓ	11.	Ⓓ
6.	Ⓒ	12.	Ⓐ

Test Practice 4
Context Clues

page 22

1.	Ⓒ	6.	Ⓓ
2.	Ⓐ	7.	Ⓓ
3.	Ⓑ	8.	Ⓑ
4.	Ⓓ	9.	Ⓐ
5.	Ⓐ	10.	Ⓓ

page 23

11.	Ⓑ	14.	Ⓒ
12.	Ⓐ	15.	Ⓐ
13.	Ⓓ	16.	Ⓓ

Test Practice 5
Main Idea and Details

page 26

1.	Ⓒ	3.	Ⓓ
2.	Ⓐ	4.	Ⓐ

page 27

5.	Ⓒ	7.	Ⓐ
6.	Ⓐ	8.	Ⓒ

Test Practice 6
Constructing Meaning

pages 30–31

1.	Ⓓ	5.	Ⓐ
2.	Ⓒ	6.	Ⓑ
3.	Ⓑ	7.	Ⓐ
4.	Ⓓ	8.	Ⓐ

Test Practice 7
Drawing Conclusions

pages 34–35

1. (A)	5. (A)
2. (C)	6. (A)
3. (B)	7. (B)
4. (D)	8. (D)

Test Practice 8
Evaluating Information

pages 38–39

1. (C)	5. (C)
2. (B)	6. (A)
3. (D)	7. (B)
4. (B)	8. (D)

Test Practice 9
Characters and Plot

pages 42–43

1. (D)	6. (B)
2. (B)	7. (A)
3. (C)	8. (D)
4. (D)	9. (B)
5. (A)	10. (B)

Test Practice 10
Reading Literature

pages 46–47

1. (C)	6. (C)
2. (D)	7. (B)
3. (A)	8. (A)
4. (B)	9. (C)
5. (A)	10. (D)

Reading Tryout Test 2

page 48

1. (C)	7. (C)
2. (A)	8. (A)
3. (B)	9. (B)
4. (D)	10. (D)
5. (C)	11. (C)
6. (D)	

page 49

12. (C)	17. (D)
13. (A)	18. (C)
14. (B)	19. (B)
15. (D)	20. (D)
16. (C)	21. (C)

page 50

22. (D)	24. (B)
23. (C)	25. (A)

pages 51–52

26. (D)	31. (A)
27. (D)	32. (C)
28. (C)	33. (B)
29. (B)	34. (A)
30. (A)	35. (C)

LANGUAGE ARTS Answers

Answer Keys

Use these answer keys to count up the number correct on each test.

Language Arts Tryout Test 1

page 55

1. Ⓐ		5. Ⓑ
2. Ⓓ		6. Ⓑ
3. Ⓓ		7. Ⓓ
4. Ⓐ		8. Ⓐ

page 56

9. Ⓒ		11. Ⓓ
10. Ⓐ		12. Ⓐ

page 57

13. Ⓒ		18. Ⓐ
14. Ⓓ		19. Ⓑ
15. Ⓑ		20. Ⓑ
16. Ⓒ		21. Ⓓ
17. Ⓐ		22. Ⓐ

page 58

23. Ⓐ		27. Ⓒ
24. Ⓒ		28. Ⓓ
25. Ⓓ		29. Ⓐ
26. Ⓑ		

page 59

30. Ⓒ		34. Ⓐ
31. Ⓒ		35. Ⓑ
32. Ⓐ		36. Ⓓ
33. Ⓓ		

Test Practice 1
Parts of Speech

page 62

1. Ⓒ		6. Ⓐ
2. Ⓓ		7. Ⓑ
3. Ⓑ		8. Ⓓ
4. Ⓒ		9. Ⓐ
5. Ⓐ		10. Ⓓ

page 63

11. Ⓓ		14. Ⓒ
12. Ⓐ		15. Ⓐ
13. Ⓓ		16. Ⓑ

Test Practice 2
Sentences

page 66

1. Ⓑ		7. Ⓒ
2. Ⓐ		8. Ⓑ
3. Ⓒ		9. Ⓑ
4. Ⓐ		10. Ⓓ
5. Ⓑ		11. Ⓒ
6. Ⓒ		12. Ⓐ

page 67

13. Ⓓ		17. Ⓓ
14. Ⓑ		18. Ⓒ
15. Ⓐ		19. Ⓒ
16. Ⓓ		20. Ⓐ

Test Practice 3
Combining Sentences

page 69

1. Ⓑ		4. Ⓐ
2. Ⓐ		5. Ⓒ
3. Ⓓ		

page 70

6. Ⓑ		9. Ⓒ
7. Ⓑ		10. Ⓓ
8. Ⓐ		

Test Practice 4
Writing Paragraphs

page 73

1. Ⓓ		3. Ⓐ
2. Ⓒ		4. Ⓓ

page 74

5. Ⓑ		7. Ⓐ
6. Ⓑ		8. Ⓑ

Test Practice 5
Spelling

page 76

1. Ⓐ	7. Ⓒ	13. Ⓑ
2. Ⓑ	8. Ⓓ	14. Ⓐ
3. Ⓒ	9. Ⓐ	15. Ⓓ
4. Ⓓ	10. Ⓓ	16. Ⓒ
5. Ⓐ	11. Ⓑ	17. Ⓐ
6. Ⓑ	12. Ⓒ	18. Ⓒ

Test Practice 5 (continued)

page 77

19.	Ⓒ	23.	Ⓐ	27.	Ⓑ
20.	Ⓑ	24.	Ⓑ	28.	Ⓑ
21.	Ⓓ	25.	Ⓓ	29.	Ⓒ
22.	Ⓒ	26.	Ⓒ	30.	Ⓐ

Test Practice 6
Punctuation

page 80

1.	Ⓒ	5.	Ⓓ
2.	Ⓐ	6.	Ⓒ
3.	Ⓐ	7.	Ⓓ
4.	Ⓑ	8.	Ⓐ

page 81

9.	Ⓒ	13.	Ⓑ
10.	Ⓐ	14.	Ⓒ
11.	Ⓓ	15.	Ⓒ
12.	Ⓑ		

Test Practice 7
Capitalization

page 83

1.	Ⓒ	7.	Ⓑ
2.	Ⓐ	8.	Ⓑ
3.	Ⓐ	9.	Ⓒ
4.	Ⓑ	10.	Ⓐ
5.	Ⓓ	11.	Ⓒ
6.	Ⓓ	12.	Ⓓ

page 84

13.	Ⓒ	17.	Ⓐ
14.	Ⓓ	18.	Ⓓ
15.	Ⓑ	19.	Ⓒ
16.	Ⓓ	20.	Ⓑ

Test Practice 8
Research Skills

page 86

1.	Ⓐ	4.	Ⓓ
2.	Ⓑ	5.	Ⓑ
3.	Ⓐ	6.	Ⓒ

Test Practice 9
Reference Sources

page 89

1.	Ⓑ	5.	Ⓒ
2.	Ⓐ	6.	Ⓒ
3.	Ⓓ	7.	Ⓓ
4.	Ⓑ	8.	Ⓑ

page 90

9.	Ⓒ	13.	Ⓓ
10.	Ⓓ	14.	Ⓐ
11.	Ⓑ	15.	Ⓒ
12.	Ⓒ		

Test Practice 10
Maps, Charts, and Graphs

page 92

1.	Ⓐ	4.	Ⓐ
2.	Ⓑ	5.	Ⓒ
3.	Ⓒ	6.	Ⓒ

page 93

7.	Ⓑ	10.	Ⓓ
8.	Ⓓ	11.	Ⓒ
9.	Ⓐ	12.	Ⓐ

Language Arts Tryout Test 2

page 94

1.	Ⓐ	5.	Ⓑ
2.	Ⓒ	6.	Ⓑ
3.	Ⓓ	7.	Ⓓ
4.	Ⓐ	8.	Ⓐ

page 95

9.	Ⓒ	11.	Ⓓ
10.	Ⓐ	12.	Ⓒ

page 96

13.	Ⓓ	18.	Ⓐ
14.	Ⓐ	19.	Ⓓ
15.	Ⓑ	20.	Ⓓ
16.	Ⓒ	21.	Ⓐ
17.	Ⓒ	22.	Ⓑ

page 97

23.	Ⓑ	27.	Ⓐ
24.	Ⓐ	28.	Ⓒ
25.	Ⓓ	29.	Ⓑ
26.	Ⓓ		

page 98

30.	Ⓑ	34.	Ⓐ
31.	Ⓓ	35.	Ⓓ
32.	Ⓐ	36.	Ⓑ
33.	Ⓑ		

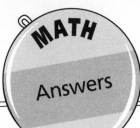
Answer Keys

Use these answer keys to count up the number correct on each test.

Math Tryout Test 1

page 101

1. Ⓒ	6. Ⓓ
2. Ⓓ	7. Ⓒ
3. Ⓐ	8. Ⓑ
4. Ⓒ	9. Ⓒ
5. Ⓑ	10. Ⓑ

page 102

11. Ⓑ	16. Ⓑ
12. Ⓐ	17. Ⓒ
13. Ⓒ	18. Ⓑ
14. Ⓓ	19. Ⓒ
15. Ⓐ	20. Ⓐ

page 103

21. Ⓒ	26. Ⓑ
22. Ⓒ	27. Ⓑ
23. Ⓐ	28. Ⓐ
24. Ⓔ	29. Ⓓ
25. Ⓓ	30. Ⓓ

page 104

31. Ⓐ	34. Ⓒ
32. Ⓔ	35. Ⓓ
33. Ⓔ	36. Ⓒ
	37. Ⓔ

page 105

38. Ⓓ	41. Ⓒ
39. Ⓒ	42. Ⓒ
40. Ⓓ	43. Ⓐ
	44. Ⓑ

Test Practice 1
Whole Number Concepts

page 108

1. Ⓒ	7. Ⓓ
2. Ⓓ	8. Ⓐ
3. Ⓑ	9. Ⓓ
4. Ⓐ	10. Ⓒ
5. Ⓒ	12. Ⓒ
6. Ⓑ	12. Ⓓ

page 109

13. Ⓑ	19. Ⓐ
14. Ⓓ	20. Ⓑ
15. Ⓒ	21. Ⓒ
16. Ⓓ	22. Ⓐ
17. Ⓓ	23. Ⓑ
18. Ⓒ	24. Ⓓ

Test Practice 2
Fractions, Decimals, and Percents

page 111

1. Ⓐ	6. Ⓑ
2. Ⓑ	7. Ⓐ
3. Ⓒ	8. Ⓓ
4. Ⓓ	9. Ⓓ
5. Ⓐ	10. Ⓒ

page 112

11. Ⓑ	17. Ⓑ
12. Ⓐ	18. Ⓓ
13. Ⓑ	19. Ⓒ
14. Ⓑ	20. Ⓓ
15. Ⓐ	21. Ⓑ
16. Ⓓ	22. Ⓐ

Test Practice 3
Computing with Whole Numbers

page 114

1. Ⓒ	7. Ⓓ
2. Ⓓ	8. Ⓓ
3. Ⓐ	9. Ⓒ
4. Ⓒ	10. Ⓑ
5. Ⓔ	12. Ⓐ
6. Ⓑ	12. Ⓔ

page 115

13. Ⓓ	19. Ⓒ
14. Ⓑ	20. Ⓔ
15. Ⓑ	21. Ⓓ
16. Ⓒ	22. Ⓒ
17. Ⓔ	23. Ⓒ
18. Ⓒ	24. Ⓐ

Test Practice 4
Computing with Fractions, Decimals, and Percents

page 117

1. Ⓒ	7. Ⓑ
2. Ⓔ	8. Ⓒ
3. Ⓐ	9. Ⓔ
4. Ⓒ	10. Ⓑ
5. Ⓓ	12. Ⓑ
6. Ⓒ	12. Ⓓ

page 118

13. Ⓔ	19. Ⓑ
14. Ⓓ	20. Ⓒ
15. Ⓐ	21. Ⓐ
16. Ⓒ	22. Ⓐ
17. Ⓔ	23. Ⓔ
18. Ⓒ	24. Ⓒ

Test Practice 5
Statistics & Probability

page 120

1.	D	5.	C
2.	A	6.	D
3.	E	7.	E
4.	A	8.	A

Test Practice 6
Problem Solving

page 123

1.	B	5.	B
2.	A	6.	C
3.	D	7.	B
4.	E	8.	E

page 124

9.	D	13.	C
10.	A	14.	D
11.	E	15.	B
12.	A	16.	A

Test Practice 7
Solving Equations and Inequalities

page 127

1.	C	7.	D
2.	B	8.	A
3.	A	9.	B
4.	E	10.	A
5.	C	11.	C
6.	A	12.	B

page 128

13.	A	17.	B
14.	D	18.	E
15.	B	19.	B
16.	D	20.	A

Test Practice 8
Geometric Figures

page 131

1.	E	4.	E
2.	A	5.	D
3.	C	6.	C

page 132

7.	E	12.	B
8.	B	13.	E
9.	D	14.	D
10.	D	15.	D
11.	C	16.	C

Test Practice 9
Measurement

page 135

1.	D	6.	A
2.	C	7.	A
3.	C	8.	C
4.	B	9.	D
5.	D	10.	B

page 136

11.	A	16.	C
12.	B	17.	B
13.	D	18.	A
14.	A	19.	C
15.	D	20.	D

Test Practice 10
Interpreting Data

page 138

1.	D	4.	B
2.	B	5.	B
3.	C	6.	C

page 139

7.	A	10.	C
8.	B	11.	D
9.	D	12.	B

Math
Tryout Test 2

page 140

1.	B	6.	B
2.	D	7.	D
3.	A	8.	C
4.	C	9.	D
5.	A	10.	A

page 141

11.	B	16.	D
12.	D	17.	B
13.	D	18.	E
14.	E	19.	B
15.	C	20.	C

page 142

21.	C	26.	C
22.	D	27.	B
23.	B	28.	A
24.	E	29.	C
25.	E	30.	D

page 143

31.	B	34.	E
32.	C	35.	D
33.	C	36.	D

page 144

37.	E	41.	C
38.	C	42.	B
39.	B	43.	C
40.	C	44.	D

Finding Percent

Number of Questions on Test

6

1	2	3	4	5	6
17%	33%	50%	67%	83%	100%

8

1	2	3	4	5	6	7	8
13%	25%	38%	50%	63%	75%	88%	100%

10

1	2	3	4	5	6	7	8	9	10
10%	20%	30%	40%	50%	60%	70%	80%	90%	100%

12

1	2	3	4	5	6	7	8	9	10	11	12
8%	17%	25%	33%	42%	50%	58%	67%	75%	83%	92%	100%

15

1	2	3	4	5	6	7	8	9	10	11	12	13	14	15
7%	13%	20%	27%	33%	40%	47%	53%	60%	67%	73%	80%	87%	93%	100%

16

1	2	3	4	5	6	7	8	9	10	11	12	13	14	15	16
6%	13%	19%	25%	31%	38%	44%	50%	56%	63%	69%	75%	81%	88%	94%	100%

20

1	2	3	4	5	6	7	8	9	10	11	12	13	14	15	16	17	18	19	20
5%	10%	15%	20%	25%	30%	35%	40%	45%	50%	55%	60%	65%	70%	75%	80%	85%	90%	95%	100%

22

1	2	3	4	5	6	7	8	9	10	11	12	13	14	15	16	17	18	19	20	21	22
5%	9%	14%	18%	23%	27%	32%	36%	41%	45%	50%	55%	59%	64%	68%	73%	77%	82%	86%	91%	95%	100%

24

1	2	3	4	5	6	7	8	9	10	11	12	13	14	15	16	17	18	19	20	21	22	23	24
4%	8%	13%	17%	21%	25%	29%	33%	38%	42%	46%	50%	54%	58%	63%	67%	71%	75%	79%	83%	88%	92%	96%	100%

30

1	2	3	4	5	6	7	8	9	10	11	12	13	14	15
3%	7%	10%	13%	17%	20%	23%	27%	30%	33%	37%	40%	43%	47%	50%

16	17	18	19	20	21	22	23	24	25	26	27	28	29	30
53%	57%	60%	63%	67%	70%	73%	77%	80%	83%	87%	90%	93%	97%	100%

35

1	2	3	4	5	6	7	8	9	10	11	12	13	14	15	16	17	18
3%	6%	9%	11%	14%	17%	20%	23%	26%	29%	31%	34%	37%	40%	43%	46%	49%	51%

19	20	21	22	23	24	25	26	27	28	29	30	31	32	33	34	35
54%	57%	60%	63%	66%	69%	71%	74%	77%	80%	83%	86%	89%	91%	94%	97%	100%

36

1	2	3	4	5	6	7	8	9	10	11	12	13	14	15	16	17	18
3%	6%	8%	11%	14%	17%	19%	22%	25%	28%	31%	33%	36%	39%	42%	44%	47%	50%

19	20	21	22	23	24	25	26	27	28	29	30	31	32	33	34	35	36
53%	56%	58%	61%	64%	67%	69%	72%	75%	78%	81%	83%	86%	89%	92%	94%	97%	100%

44

1	2	3	4	5	6	7	8	9	10	11	12	13	14	15	16	17	18	19
2%	5%	7%	9%	11%	14%	16%	18%	20%	23%	25%	27%	30%	32%	34%	36%	39%	41%	43%

20	21	22	23	24	25	26	27	28	29	30	31	32	33	34	35	36	37	38	39	40	41	42	43	44
45%	48%	50%	52%	55%	57%	59%	61%	64%	66%	68%	70%	73%	75%	77%	80%	82%	84%	86%	89%	91%	93%	95%	98%	100%